D0684659

FINDING GRACE
AT THE CENTER

DISCARDED

**Other SkyLight Paths books
by M. Basil Pennington, OCSO**

*The Monks of Mount Athos:
A Western Monk's Extraordinary Spiritual Journey
on Eastern Holy Ground*

*Psalms:
A Spiritual Commentary*

*The Song of Songs:
A Spiritual Commentary*

FINDING GRACE AT THE CENTER, 3RD EDITION

THE BEGINNING OF CENTERING PRAYER

M. BASIL PENNINGTON, OCSO

THOMAS KEATING, OCSO

THOMAS E. CLARKE, SJ

FOREWORD BY REV. CYNTHIA BOURGEAULT, PHD

Walking Together, Finding the Way®

SKYLIGHT PATHS®
PUBLISHING

Woodstock, Vermont

www.skylightpaths.com

Finding Grace at the Center, 3rd. Ed.:
The Beginning of Centering Prayer

2009 Quality Paperback Third Edition, Second Printing
2007 Quality Paperback Third Edition, First Printing
© 2007 Third Edition by the Cistercian Abbey of Spencer, Inc.
Foreword © 2007 by Rev. Cynthia Bourgeault, PhD

First published 1978 by Saint Bede's Publications

All rights reserved. No part of this book may be reproduced or transmitted in any form or by any means, electronic or mechanical, including photocopying, recording, or by any information storage and retrieval system, without permission in writing from the publisher.

For information regarding permission to reprint material from this book, please mail or fax your request in writing to SkyLight Paths Publishing, Permissions Department, at the address / fax number listed below, or e-mail your request to permissions@skylightpaths.com.

The Library of Congress has cataloged the first edition as follows:

Pennington, M. Basil.

Finding grace at the center : the beginning of centering prayer / M. Basil Pennington, Thomas Keating, Thomas E. Clarke.
p.   cm.
Originally published: Still River, Mass.: St. Bede Publications, c1978.
Includes bibliographical references.
ISBN-13: 978-1-893361-69-0 (hardcover)
ISBN-10: 1-893361-69-1 (hardcover)
1. Contemplation. I. Keating, Thomas. II. Clarke, Thomas E. III. Title.
BV5091.C7 .P465 2002
248.3—dc21

2002005568

ISBN-13: 978-1-59473-182-2 (quality pbk.)
ISBN-10: 1-59473-182-9 (quality pbk.)

10 9 8 7 6 5 4 3 2

Manufactured in the United States of America

Cover design: Bridgett Taylor

SkyLight Paths, "Walking Together, Finding the Way" and colophon are trademarks of LongHill Partners, Inc. registered in the U.S. Patent and Trademark Office.

Walking Together, Finding the Way®
Published by SkyLight Paths Publishing
A Division of Longhill Partners, Inc.
Sunset Farm Offices, Route 4, P.O. Box 237
Woodstock, VT 05091
Tel: (802) 457-4000   Fax: (802) 457-4004
www.skylightpaths.com

**Grateful acknowledgment is made
to the following for permission to use
previously copyrighted material:**

"Centering Prayer—Prayer of Quiet"
originally appeared in *Cross and Crown*, March 1977.
Reprinted with permission of the copyright holder.

"Cultivating the Centering Prayer"
based on an article originally appearing in
Review for Religious, January 1978.
Reprinted with permission. All rights reserved.
Copyright 1978 by Review for Religious,
539 N. Grand Blvd., St. Louis, Missouri 63103

"Contemplative Prayer in Christian Tradition"
reprinted with permission of *America*. All rights reserved.
Copyright 1978 by America Press, Inc.,
106 W. 56th St., New York, NY 10019

"Finding Grace at the Center"
reprinted with permission from *The Way.*

"Focus on Centering Prayer"
reprinted with permission from *In-formation.*

CONTENTS

FOREWORD TO THE THIRD EDITION

This book takes us back to the headwaters, to the very beginnings of what may well be one of the most significant spiritual awakenings of the twentieth century. Some thirty years ago, in a cloistered Trappist monastery near Spencer, Massachusetts, hearts were suddenly on fire as a trio of monks—Abbot Thomas Keating, Fr. William Meninger, and Fr. Basil Pennington—discovered it was possible to put "the essence of the Christian contemplative tradition" into a simple and easily accessible form of meditation responsive to the spiritual hunger of the times. Called "Centering Prayer," or "the Centering Prayer," the practice was first taught quietly to small groups of clergy, monks, and nuns on retreat at the monastery. Then the floodgates burst and Centering Prayer spread like wildfire: to Catholic laity ... to Protestants ... across North America ... and throughout the world.

In 1978, about three years into that revolution, Thomas Keating and Basil Pennington teamed up with Thomas Clarke, a Jesuit priest and early practitioner of the prayer, for the first attempt to gather the emerging teachings in book-length form. This is the book you now hold in your hands. It is one of the original pieces of writing to emerge from the Centering Prayer movement and it offers a fascinating glimpse of both a moment in time and a timeless moment.

Beginner's mind is always a wondrous thing. If you are presently a practitioner of Centering Prayer, try to imagine yourself back in a time before any of those well-turned teaching phrases had yet been formulated: "twenty minutes, twice a day"; "return ever so gently to the Sacred Word"; "the fruits of this prayer are to be found in daily life." Here you see the teaching taking shape before your eyes. What shines through these early efforts is the remarkable mutuality with which Frs. Keating and Pennington share in the midwifing of this new prayer form. Each contributes from his own rich store of spiritual experience the images, core metaphors, and practical instructions that, even now, are standard fare in Centering Prayer introductory workshops.

As the Centering Prayer movement developed, these founding fathers eventually went their own ways—not through any animosity, but simply due to the inevitable drift of two highly creative and original minds carving their own paths. Not long after *Finding Grace at the Center* made its appearance, Basil and Thomas each wrote and published full length books of their own: Basil's *Centering Prayer: Renewing an Ancient Christian Prayer Form* in 1980,[1] and Thomas's *Open Mind, Open Heart* in 1986. By the time I became involved with the movement in the late 1980s, the "Keating school" and "Pennington school" of Centering Prayer were already distinct streams—complementary, but with decidedly different flavors.

More and more, Thomas Keating came to see the future of the contemplative reawakening as lying beyond the monastery walls. In 1984 he founded Contemplative Outreach, Ltd., a national membership organization to provide training and ongoing support for an emerging network of lay contemplatives (today its membership is close to 50,000). His prolific writings

---

[1] Technically, Basil's earliest work, *Daily We Touch Him*, had already just been published by Doubleday in 1977. It was later revised and republished as *Daily We Touch Him: Practical Religious Experiences* (Kansas City: Sheed and Ward, 1997).

and videotape lectures became geared toward re-presenting this ancient monastic art in terms (and media formats) readily accessible to modern spiritual seekers. Drawing extensively on the insights of contemporary psychology, he developed his innovative teachings on the false self system and the Divine Therapy as a new roadmap for the spiritual journey. Today, well into his eighties, he continues to grow in both the range of his interests and the sphere of his influence. Among Keating's recent involvements, he has teamed up with the Dalai Lama to explore the emerging field of neuromeditation and with Ken Wilber to help launch the Integral Institute. He has emerged more and more in recent years as a planetary citizen, no doubt the most widely recognized Christian spokesperson for an emerging universal spiritual consciousness of our times.

While an equally gifted teacher and prolific writer, Basil's course over the next three decades stayed closer to his monastic wellsprings. The early good fortune of having published his first book with the prestigious Doubleday house established him in the eyes of the literary public as the "official" spokesperson for Centering Prayer. He held the post gracefully, making his annual rounds as a much-sought-after speaker and retreat leader. But inwardly, his spiritual compass became more and more settled within his own Trappist orbit.

During the 1980s and 1990s he spent extended sojourns with the monks in Ava, Missouri, and then with the Trappists in China. Finally, his heart found its home when he was called in 1999 as abbot of Our Lady of the Holy Spirit in Conyers, Georgia. His long journey with Centering Prayer had deepened his understanding of his own monastic heritage, and he yearned to share his passion for a radical renewal of the monastic life.

In their teachings as well, so closely interwoven at the start, these two spiritual giants would eventually develop some significant nuances, particularly in their respective understandings of the use of the Sacred Word. As you'll see in this book, both of them emphasize the original instructions in *The Cloud of Unknowing* that the Sacred Word should be "personally meaningful." But, over time, Basil's commitment to this instruction grew, while Thomas's diminished. Basil remained anchored in the traditional Christian understanding that contemplative prayer arises out of a "suffusion of affectivity"—or, in other words, out of a personal love for God so concentrated and transfigured that it "implodes" into silence. While Thomas initially assented to this understanding, over time he moved more and more in the direction of seeing the Word as simply the vehicle for a person's intention to "consent to the presence and action of God," and his teaching moved beyond the classic tradition toward a pure kenotic (self-emptying) mysticism—still fully within the parameters of Christian orthodoxy, but definitely the road less traveled.

All in all, then, it would be fair to say that Basil took the more conservative course—by "conservative" I intend the highest sense of the word (that is, deeply loyal to a living tradition), not the implications of narrowness and rigidity that the term so often conveys. For Basil's vision was anything but narrow. He was broadly inclusive and welcoming, and his gifts as a pastor and practical teacher were always front and center. In all his writings you will hear that voice of encouragement and common sense, which makes the challenge of taking up a contemplative practice in the midst of daily life seem somehow doable. So much of his original vision and terminology, including his emphasis on simplicity and gentleness, have become part of the enduring legacy of the Centering Prayer movement.

Unfortunately, gentleness was not to be the outcome of his own spiritual journey—at least not as we know it from this side. The final three years of his life were marked by a series of abrupt and bitter reversals. In 2002 he was asked to resign as abbot of Conyers (in part because his zeal for a sweeping reconstitution of the monastic life outpaced his patience for building consensus among his monastic brethren). Returning home to Spencer, he continued with his writing and spiritual correspondence. In February, 2005, he sustained fatal injuries in an automobile crash and, after six weeks of what can only be imagined as inner and outer purgatory, made the decision to discontinue life supports. He died on June 3, 2005—an unexpected and untimely end to a life of incredible dedication and spiritual force.

His colleague Thomas Keating spoke honestly and courageously at his funeral, reminding those present that the fruit of the contemplative journey is total transformation, and that in service of this total transformation, sometimes "the best use of one's talents is to give them up." Not advice for the spiritually immature; nor did Thomas nuance his message by saying, "give up *attachment* to your talents." But surely Basil would have understood and been honored by the subtle innuendo here. For the contemplative journey, at least as lived by its most committed and valiant truth-seekers, amounts to no less than an ongoing divine alchemy. The outer shell of personality, achievements, and talents is to be continuously offered up ("in the holocaust of becoming," as my own spiritual teacher, Brother Raphael, used to say) to reveal what lies at the core. In the end, all that is not God is burned away, and the transfiguring fire of Divine love glows through the fragile contours of a human form like the bush that burns but is not consumed. To that path, the inner monasticism of total transformation in God, Basil bent his life and his works, as will we all, if we follow this path to its end.

It is fitting then, as this new edition of *Finding Grace at the Center* makes its appearance, to pause and remember Basil in a special way: an exuberant, larger-than-life man with a full white beard, flowing monastic robes, and a passion for sharing God through contemplative prayer. With his unique gifts of practicality, accessibility, and clarity, he introduced thousands to the path; his encouragement and boundless enthusiasm still shine forth, no less brightly than when the book first made its appearance nearly thirty years ago. May our return to the wellsprings bring with it a fresh appreciation for his enduring legacy.

Rev. Cynthia Bourgeault, PhD
Director, The Aspen Wisdom School

FOREWORD TO THE 25TH ANNIVERSARY EDITION

Welcome. It is just twenty-five years since this first book on Centering Prayer was published. In that short time this simple, traditional way of prayer has been taught and practiced in all parts of the world, from Korea to New Zealand, Beijing to Moscow, South Africa to Norway, all across the United States and Latin America. It is as though a parched earth was awaiting the first spring rain. Minds and hearts were open and ready to receive.

Religious took the lead, with the Leadership Conference of Religious Women joining up with the Conference of Major Superiors of Men to bring this ancient gift to their membership. The National Conference of Catholic Bishops was not slow to follow, inviting us to share the prayer with them in their annual meeting. In 1984 the Contemplative Outreach was organized to develop lay leadership in the Centering Prayer movement and the Mastery Foundation to help those whose lives are about sacred ministry to ground themselves with contemplative prayer.

In the list of resources at the end of this edition you will see some of the books, audiotapes, and videotapes that have been published in these years in the English language. To these might be added lists of translations: Spanish, Italian, French, German, Japanese, Chinese, and many other languages. Later this year a group of Centering Prayer books will be published in Poland. Programs, courses, and seminars, as well as retreats, parish days and Eleventh-step Groups, have been offered. In the fall 2002 semester, Centering Prayer will be taught at Harvard.

A very precious part of our Christian heritage has been re-found. And many are the stories that could be told about the difference daily Centering has made in the lives of men and women—young and old, rich and poor—and children, too. Centering Prayer has been the source of many vocations to priestly and religious life and the mainstay of many others.

In the course of the years, sitting in silent prayer, beyond where words can interfere, men and women of many diverse traditions have come together. In that deeper place a oneness is experienced that gives assurance and heart to our feeble ecumenical efforts and our interreligious dialogues.

Maharishi Mahesh Yogi has said that if one percent of the people would meditate we will have peace. Jesus spoke of the leaven that will leaven the whole. We have seen it happen in South Africa where Centering Prayer played its quiet but effective role as apartheid came to an end and Boards of Reconciliation appeared.

This slim volume continues to be a vehicle for that leaven. These initial articles have a simplicity about them that gives them an effective clarity. They will continue to be for many the first place they come into contact with this rich vein of our ancient Christian heritage, very old but ever new. We are grateful to the Benedictine nuns of Saint Scholastica's Abbey, Petersham, Massachusetts, who first put this volume together and made it available to the public. And we are now grateful to Jon Sweeney and all at SkyLight Paths for once again assuring its effective availability. Whether you are new to Centering Prayer or have long been enjoying it, I am sure you will find the savoring of these early essays a pleasure and a profitable one.

M. Basil Pennington, OCSO
Our Lady of the Holy Spirit Abbey
Conyers, Georgia 30094

FOREWORD TO THE FIRST EDITION

St. John of the Cross tells us there are many people who think they are praying when they are not, and there are others who think they are not praying when they are. We also learn from Holy Scripture that ideas on prayer are apt to be strange (as described in Chapter 6 of St. Matthew, for example). Since there is a growing interest in prayer today, it is important to find the right answers to the questions that are commonly asked: "What is prayer? Why should I pray? What is contemplation?" The answers to questions like these are often difficult to find, bewildering at best. Many, therefore, decide that the whole subject of prayer is too complex after all and is not meant for them. They end by sympathizing with Dom John Chapman who said that all spiritual writers disagreed with one another and that he disagreed with all of them. To help such searchers, it was decided to publish these articles, written by an abbot and two priests—all contemplatives and spiritual masters, familiar with the needs and aspirations of our time.

These authors emphasize the fact that since everyone is called to eternal beatitude, everyone is called to contemplation. St. Teresa' of Ávila and St. John of the Cross teach this explicitly. The latter, in his writings on mystical prayer, addressed himself "to one and all, provided they have made up their mind to pass through nakedness of spirit." Abbot Thomas Keating reiterates this when he says that "contemplation is the normal evolution of a genuine spiritual life and hence open to all Christians."

This, of course, is not to say that contemplation for a Christian is an end in itself. It can be a purely intellectual exercise in the Aristotelian or Platonic sense where the soul focuses on certain values like goodness or being in an effort to reach the highest understanding of these values. Or it can be a sort of exercise in negative contemplation in which the soul, realizing that all knowledge is defective, tries to transcend it by emptying the mind of all knowledge.

The highest kind of Christian prayer, though it may presuppose these two exercises and incorporate their methodology, goes vastly beyond them. This is what St. John of the Cross calls spiritual marriage; our perfect union in love with God through Christ, based on the realization that this God whom we can know, though defectively, through our concepts and human values, and who infinitely transcends them and, therefore, remains ineffable, has revealed Himself in the Scriptures and even more intensely in the mysteries of His Incarnation and death engendered by love alone. This union, this face-to-face encounter, this "kiss of the mouth," in the words of the Canticle of Canticles, is a sharing in the life of the Trinity. We become, in fact, so immersed in the Trinity, that St. John of the Cross does not hesitate to say that the Holy Spirit, the mutual "breath" of Father and Son, becomes the mutual "breath" of God and the soul. If anyone is frightened by these concepts, he should understand they are resolved by love. Both the Old and the New Testaments describe God's relationship to us as that of a lover, and our response to Him as the response of a beloved. The transcendent, "immutable" God makes Himself vulnerable for love of us. As Father Basil Pennington says, "that is the one thing for which He created us, and which gives us our infinite importance and worth, our personal love. No one else can give God our personal love." No one can say he is incapable of love. It is as natural as breathing whether we consider the act or the object.

These articles, therefore, have a lot to say to everyone. They cannot say everything—the subject of prayer is too vast. But they explain the broad outlines, answer questions, suggest the parameters, point out the possibilities to be reached and the pitfalls to be avoided.

S. M. Clare

FINDING GRACE AT THE CENTER

CENTERING PRAYER

M. BASIL PENNINGTON, OCSO

Over the years in retreat work I have talked to many, many priests and religious. I have found that in most cases, though not all, in the seminary or in the novitiate they have been taught methods of prayer and active meditation. In many cases they have also had a course in ascetical or mystical theology in which they have heard about the various stages of contemplative prayer. Unfortunately they have usually been left with the impression or have been actually taught that it is a very rare sort of thing, usually found only in enclosed monasteries. To seek it is presumptuous. One must plug away faithfully in active meditation and perhaps some day, in the far distant future, after long years of fidelity, God might give one this precious but rare gift of contemplative prayer. Rarely have I found anyone who had been taught in the seminary or the novitiate a simple method for entering into passive meditation or contemplative prayer.

This is sad. Especially in face of the fact that St. Teresa of Ávila had taught that those who were faithful to prayer could expect in a relatively short time—six months or a year—to be led into a prayer of quiet. Dom Marmion believed that by the end of the novitiate, a religious was usually ready for contemplative prayer. One of the signs that St. John of the Cross pointed to as an indication that one is ready for contemplative prayer is that active meditation no longer works—an experience very many priests and religious do have. Faced with this experience, and with no one showing them how to move on to contemplative prayer, many give up regular prayer. A faithful few plug on, sometimes for years, making painful meditations that are anything but refreshing. Given this state of affairs, it is not surprising that Christians seeking help to enter into this quiet, inner experience of God have found little among their priests and religious. In the 1960s and 1970s such seekers not infrequently turned to the East.

A Challenge from the East

If a person desiring to seek the experience of God in deep meditation does go to one of the many swamis found in the West today, he or she will be quickly taught a simple method to pursue this goal. "Sit this way. Hold your hands this way. Breathe thus. Say the word in this manner. Do this twice a day for so many minutes." And if the recipient does this, he or she usually has very good experiences. We can see this, up to a point, as a good thing. In carrying through this exercise, devoting mind and heart to this pursuit, the seeker is actually engaging in a very pure form of prayer. The sad part of it is that his pursuit and his experience of God's very real presence in him in his creative love is not clearly integrated with his faith. Sadder still is the fact that, in some cases, grateful recipients, so helped by the swami's meditation technique, have accepted from him, also, his philosophy of life, abandoning their Christian heritage. Some of the greater swamis, such as Swami Satchidananda and Maharishi Mahesh Yogi, certainly advise against this, but such advice can fall on ears deafened by an almost cultic veneration for a truly selfless master.

These good masters from the East are truly a challenge, whether they intend to be or not, and in more ways than one. For one thing they certainly remind us that the effective teacher, at least in the area of life-giving teaching, must be one who lives what he teaches. To try to teach the Christian gospel with its strong bias for the poor and its way of daily abnegation—"If you would be my disciple, take up your cross daily (not monthly or weekly, my novice master would say with emphasis, but daily) and come follow me" (Luke 9:23)—and still to be busy pursuing the same pleasures and immediate goals as the worldly materialist is to condemn oneself to a fruitless ministry. We must teach more by what we do and how we live than by what we say, if we want our hearers to take us seriously.

A Response to This Challenge

The current appeal of the swamis makes us ask ourselves, are there not in our own Christian tradition some simple methods, some meditation techniques, which we can use to open the way to quiet, contemplative union with God? Before responding, I would like to say that we Christians should not hesitate to make use of the good techniques that our wise friends from the East are offering, if we find them, in fact, helpful. As St. Paul said: "All things are yours, and you are Christ's and Christ is God's" (1 Cor. 3:23). We should not hesitate to take the fruit of the age-old wisdom of the East and "capture" it for Christ. Indeed, those of us who are in ministry should make the necessary effort to acquaint ourselves with as many of these Eastern techniques as possible. Not that we will necessarily find them useful in our own prayer seeking, though that might be the case, but that we might be prepared to enter into intelligent dialogue with Eastern spiritual masters and, more important, that we might be prepared to help our fellow Christians, who do learn these techniques and find them helpful, to integrate them into their Christian faith experience. Many Christians who take their prayer life seriously have been greatly helped by Yoga, Zen, TM, and similar practices, especially where they have been initiated by reliable teachers and have a solidly developed Christian faith to give inner form and meaning to the resulting experiences.

But to return to our question: Do we have, in our Christian tradition, simple methods or techniques for opening the way to contemplative prayer? Yes, we certainly do. Some might draw back at this statement. The idea of using a "technique" to communicate with God, whom we have the privilege of knowing personally, seems repulsive. And to expect to attain to contemplation by a "technique" smacks of Pelagianism. So let me explain.

The Use of "Techniques"

First of all, "techniques," methods, are certainly not foreign to the prayer experience of the average Catholic. The Rosary is a "technique"—and certainly not one to be readily discounted. It has led many, many Christians to deep contemplative union with God. The Stations of the Cross are another "technique." So are the Ignatian exercises, which are directly ordered to contemplation. Well enough known in the West today, at least by name and reputation, is the ancient Eastern Christian technique of the Jesus Prayer. We have, in fact, many Christian techniques.

The use of a technique or method in prayer to help us come into contact with God present to us, in us, and to bring our whole selves into quietness to enjoy that presence and be refreshed by it, is certainly not, in itself Pelagian. Mystical theologians have not hesitated to speak of an *acquired* contemplation—in distinction to *infused* contemplation—a contemplative state or experience which the contemplator has taken some part in bringing into being. All prayer is a response to God and begins with Him. To deny this would be Pelagian. It is not only in infused contemplation that God's grace is operative. When the little child lisps his "Now I lay me down to sleep...," if there is any movement of faith and love there, any true prayer, grace is present and operative. Every prayer is a response to a movement of grace, whether we are explicitly aware of it or not, whether we consciously experience the movement, the call, the attraction, or not. God present in us, present all around us, is calling us to respond to His presence, His love, His caring. We are missing reality if we think otherwise.

When we use a technique, a method, to pray, we are doing so because God's grace, to which we are freely responding, is efficaciously inviting us to do this. That we have been taught the technique and have responded to the teaching is all part of His grace at work, inviting us, leading us, guiding us to a deeper experience of our union with Him. That is why it takes a certain courage—or foolhardiness—to learn such a technique. For it is, indeed, an invitation from the Lord to enter and abide within. Not to respond to such a loving invitation from the infinite God of love is sheer tragedy. Yet, to respond to such an invitation is to open oneself to a transformation of conscience and consciousness, with all that that can lead to. One's life will never be the same again.

The Prayer of "The Cloud"

Yes, we do have in our Christian tradition simple methods, "techniques," for entering into contemplative prayer, a prayer of quiet. And without more ado I would like to share one such method with you. The one I have chosen is drawn from a little volume called *The Cloud of Unknowing*,[1] which is indeed a popular book in our time. The author is an unknown English Catholic writer of the fourteenth century. He could hardly have put his name to the work, for all that it teaches belongs to the common heritage of the Christian community.

At the time of our author's writing there was a vibrant spirituality alive and widespread in the Christian West. The swell had begun with the Gregorian reform in the eleventh century and the ensuing monastic revival. The great Cistercian abbeys of the twelfth century often housed

---

[1] At present *The Cloud of Unknowing* is available in four paperback editions, the best of which is that translated by William Johnson, SJ, and published by Doubleday & Co. When quoted in this article, this work will be referred to parenthetically in the text as C, followed by the appropriate chapter number. [Editor's Note: Several more editions of *The Cloud of Unknowing* are now available, but the Johnson translation remains a favorite.]

only eighty or a hundred monks, but had hundreds of lay brothers who labored in the granges, opening up new land or developing sheep runs, or who were active in the markets and agricultural trading centers. These men were not unlike the figure of the starets made familiar to us by the novels of Dostoevski. While they shared their agricultural concerns with the hired help, the neighboring peasants and serfs, or sold their wool in the markets, they did not fail to share at the same time something of their spiritual awareness and their simple ways of prayer. These holy men were followed by the enthusiastic sons of St. Francis and the other mendicant orders. All, even the poorest, the most illiterate, were invited to intimacy with the Lord. The fourteenth century was a high tide for the Christian spirit in the West.

Unfortunately it would soon enough ebb. With the Reformation, the monastic centers of spiritual life would be swept away by the new currents that flowed through much of Europe. And on the rest of the continent the prosecution of Quietism and Illuminism by an overly zealous and defensive Inquisition would send contemplation to hide fearfully in the corners of a few convents and monasteries. A great movement of the Christian spirit flowed away with the undercurrent, only to surface and return under the impulsion of the mighty winds of a Second Pentecost. These winds blow across the face of the whole earth. They certainly are not contained by the Church. But the Church, the Christian community, cannot afford to be slow to respond to them. True renewal must begin with each Christian, responding to the call of the Spirit within, to the call to the center where God dwells, waiting to refresh, revitalize, renew.

This simple method of entering into contemplative prayer has been aptly called *centering prayer*. The name is inspired by Thomas Merton. In his writings he stressed that the simplest way to come into contact with the living God is to go to one's center and from there pass into God. This is the way the author of *The Cloud* would lead us, although his imagery is somewhat different.

The simple method he teaches really belongs to the common heritage of man. I remember on one occasion describing it to a teacher of Transcendental Meditation. He replied, "Why, that's TM." I could not agree with him. There are very significant differences, but perhaps it really takes faith to perceive them. I can also remember, when I was in Greece, finding a Greek translation of *The Cloud of Unknowing*. The late Archbishop of Corinth had written the introduction. In it he stated that this was the work of an unknown fourteenth century, English, *Orthodox* writer. He was certain it belonged to his Christian tradition.

If one reads *The Cloud* on his own, as perhaps many of my readers have, he is not likely to draw from the text the simple technique the author offers. This is not to be wondered at. One will have the same experience reading books on the Jesus Prayer. As the spiritual fathers on Mount Athos pointed out to me, no spiritual father would seek to teach the Jesus Prayer by a book. It is meant to be handed on personally—by tradition. The writings are but to support the learner in his experience and help him place the practice in the full context of his life. This, too, I believe is the case with *The Cloud of Unknowing*. Simply reading it will not usually teach the method.

For this reason I shall try to spell out the "technique" of *The Cloud* in a concrete manner, adding some practical advice and explanation. To do this I shall sum up the method in three rules. But first let me say a word about posture and relaxation.

Posture and Relaxation

Some wonderful ways of sitting have come to us from the East. They are ideal for meditation. But unless we are long practiced, and in most cases, having gotten an early start, our muscles and bones do not too readily adapt themselves to these postures. I think that for most of us Westerners the best posture for prayer is to be comfortably settled in a good chair—one that gives firm support to the back, but at the same time is not too hard or stiff. As the author of *The Cloud* says, "Simply sit relaxed and quiet...."

Most important, the body should be relaxed. When our Lord said, "Come to me all you who labor and are heavily burdened, and I will refresh you" (Matt. 11:28), He meant the whole man: body, soul, and spirit—not just the spirit. But the body is not apt to be refreshed if we begin the prayer physically tense. Settling down in our chair and letting go, letting the chair fully support the body, is sacramental of what is to take place in the prayer. In centering prayer we settle in God, let ourselves go, let him fully support us, rest us, refresh us.

Posture and relaxation are important. It is good, too, if we close our eyes during this prayer. It is true, some techniques like Zen call for keeping the eyes open. But these are usually effortful techniques. This method, however, is effortless; it is a letting go. "It is simply a spontaneous desire, springing from God..." (C, chap. 4). The more we can gently eliminate outside disturbances the better.

That is why it is good, if possible, to make this prayer in a quiet place, a place apart, though this is not essential. More important is it that it be a situation in which we will not be disturbed in the course of the meditation. I have meditated this way in airports—certainly not quiet places, but no one will ordinarily disturb you as you sit there among the many waiting passengers. Quiet, though, will usually be found helpful. Psychologically, also, it is experienced as helpful if one has a sort of special place for meditation—a place apart, even though "apart" may be only a corner of a room where there is a presence sacramentalized in Bible, icon, or sacred image, and the going apart simply involves swinging around in our chair from desk to shrine. The physical set-up and the bodily movement reinforce the sense of passing now from the frenetic activities of the day to a deeper state of prayerful rest and divine refreshment.

Three Rules

But now let us get on with the "rules" for entering into centering prayer, the prayer of quiet, contemplation.

One: At the beginning of the prayer we take a minute or two to quiet down and then move in faith and love to God dwelling in our depths; and at the end of the prayer we take several minutes to come out, mentally praying the Our Father.

So, once we are settled down in our chair and relaxed, we enter into a short period of silence. Sixty seconds can initially seem like a long time when we are doing nothing and are used to being constantly on the go. Better to take a little more time rather than less.

Then we move in faith to God, Father, Son, and Holy Spirit, dwelling in creative love in the depths of our being. This is the whole essence of the prayer. "Center all your attention and desire on Him and let this be the sole concern of your mind and heart" (C, chap. 3). Faith moving towards its Object in hope and love—this is the whole of the theological, the Christian life. All the rest of the method is simply a means to enable us to abide quietly in this center, and to allow our whole being to share in this refreshing contact with its Source.

Faith is fundamental for this prayer, as for any prayer. We will have no desire to enter into union and communion, to pray, if we do not have at least some glimmer in faith of the All-Lovable, the All-Desirable. But it is more especially a "wonderful work of love," a response to Him who is known by living faith.

The Inner Presence

When God makes things, He does not just put them together and toss them out there, to let them fly alone in His creation. "One is good—God" (Matt. 19:17). And One is true, and beautiful, and all being—our God. Everything else *is* only in so far as it here and now actively participates in Him and shares His being. At every moment God is intimately present to each and every particle of His creation, sharing with it, in creative love, His very own being. If we really see this book, we do not just see the book, but we see God bringing it into being and sustaining it in being. We perceive the divine presence.

If this is true of all the other elements, how much more true is it for the greatest of God's creation—man, made to His very own image and likeness. When we go to our depths we find not only the image of God, but God Himself, bringing us forth in His creative love. We go to our center and pass from there into the present God.

Yet there is still something even more wonderful here. We have been baptized into Christ. We are in some very real, though mysterious way, Christ, the Son of God, the Second Person of the Blessed Trinity. "I live, now not I, but Christ lives in me" (Gal. 2:20). As we go to the depths we realize in faith our identity with Christ the Son. And even now, with Him and in Him, we come forth from the Father in the eternal generation, and return to the Father in that perfect Love which is the Holy Spirit. What prayer! This is really stupendous, beyond adequate conception. Yet our faith tells us it is so. It is part of that whole reality that revelation has opened up to us. And it is for us to take possession of it. We have been made sharers in the divine nature by baptism. We have been given the gift of the Holy Spirit. We have but to enter into what is ours, what we truly are.

And that is what we do in this prayer. In a movement of faith that includes hope and love, we go to the center and turn ourselves over to God in a simple "being there," in a presence that is perfect and complete adoration, response, love, and "Amen" to that movement that we are in the Son to the Father. That is what St. Paul was talking about when he said, "We do not know how to pray as we ought, but the Spirit Himself prays for us..." (Rom. 8:26).

Coming Out of Contemplation

In this prayer we go very deep into ourselves. Some speak of a fourth state of consciousness, a state beyond waking, sleeping, or dreaming states. Tests have shown that meditators do achieve a state of rest which is deeper than that attained in sleep. Have you ever had the experience of being suddenly rudely awakened out of very deep sleep? It is rather jarring, to say the least. We do not want to come out of contemplative prayer in a jarring way. Rather we want to bring its deep peace into the whole of our life. That is why we prescribe taking several minutes coming out, moving from the level of deep, self-forgetful contemplation to silent awareness and then a conscious interior prayer, before moving out into full activity. When the time we have determined to pray is completed, we stop using the prayer word, savor the silence, the Presence, for a bit, and then begin interiorly to pray the Our Father.

I suggest saying the Our Father. It is a perfect prayer, taught us by the Lord Himself. We gently let the successive phrases come to mind. We savor them, enter into them. What matter if in fact it takes a good while. It is a beginning of letting our contemplative prayer flow out into the rest of our lives. Other favorite prayers can be used, or we can pray spontaneously in our own words.

A Valuable Asceticism

We strongly recommend two periods of contemplative prayer in the course of a day. The first, in the morning, introduces into our day a good rhythm: a period of deep rest and refreshment in the Lord flowing out into eight or ten hours of fruitful activity. The second is a period of renewal to carry us through, what is for almost everyone today, a long evening of activity. This is certainly much better than trying to base sixteen hours of activity on the morning prayer.

Twenty minutes seems to be a good period to start with. Less than this hardly gives one a chance to get fully into the prayer and be wholly refreshed. Some will feel themselves drawn to extend the period to twenty-five or thirty minutes or perhaps thirty-five. On a day of retreat or when we are sick in bed, and our activity is curtailed, we can easily add more periods of contemplative prayer. This might be better than prolonging individual periods. Those who are living a contemplative life may find somewhat longer periods helpful.

For most of us, the real asceticism of this form of prayer comes in scheduling into our daily life two periods for it. Once we are going full steam, it is difficult to stop, drop everything, go apart and simply be to the Lord. And yet there is a tremendous value here.

All of us theoretically subscribe to the word of the Psalmist: "Unless the Lord build the house, in vain the masons toil" (Ps. 127:1). But in practice most of us work as though God could not possibly get things done if we did not do them for Him. The fact is there is nothing that we are doing that God could not raise up a stone in the field to do for Him. The realization of this puts us in our true place. Though, lest we do get too knocked down by such a realization of our insignificance, let me hasten to add that there is one thing that we alone can give God. And that is the one thing for which He created us, and which gives us our infinite importance and worth, and that one thing is our personal love. No one else can give God our personal love. It is uniquely for this that He created us. This is our great significance. The very God of heaven and earth wants, and needs because He wants, our personal love.

Yes, we theoretically subscribe to the truth that God is the principal agent. But we push frenetically on. Nothing can help us so much to get a real grasp on the fact of God's allness in our accomplishments—and the peace and freedom that come from such a practical realization—as actually stopping regularly and letting God take care of things. He really can! We can trust Him to manage His world for twenty minutes without us while we meditate!

And if, while we pray, some may have to wait at our door for ten or fifteen minutes, they will probably learn a lot about prayer while they wait—certainly more than if they were inside listening to us talk about prayer.

Actions speak louder than words. Those around us will not fail to notice, even though we might prefer they would not, when we begin to give prayer prime time in our busy lives.

> Two: After resting for a bit in the Presence in faith-full love, we take up a single, simple word that expresses our response and begin to let it repeat itself within.

As the author of *The Cloud* puts it: "If you want to gather all your desire into one simple word that the mind can easily retain, choose a short word rather than a long one. A one-syllable word such as *God* or *love* is best. But choose one that is meaningful to you. Then fix it in your mind so that it will remain there, come what may.... Be careful in this work and never strain your mind or imagination, for truly you will not succeed in this way. Leave these faculties at peace" (C, chaps. 4 & 7).

What we are concerned with here is a simple, effortless prolongation or abiding in the act of faith—love—presence. This is so simple, so effortless, so restful, that it is a bit subtle and so needs some explanation.

A spiritual act is an instantaneous act, an act without time. "The will needs only this brief fraction of a moment to move toward the object of its desires" (C, chap. 4). As soon as we move in love to God present in our depths, we are there. There a perfect prayer of adoration, love, and presence is. And we simply want to remain there and be what we are: Christ responding to the Father in the perfect Love, the Holy Spirit.

To facilitate our abiding quietly there, and to bring our whole being as much as possible to rest in this abiding, after a brief experience of silent presence we take up a single, simple word that expresses for us our faith-love movement. We have seen that the author of *The Cloud* suggests such words as *God* or *love*. A vocative word seems usually to be best. We begin very simply to let this word repeat itself within us. We let it take its own pace, louder or softer, faster or slower; it may even fuzz out into silence. "It is best when this word is wholly interior without a definite thought or actual sound" (C, chap. 4).

We might think of it as if the Lord Himself, present in our depths, were quietly repeating His own name, evoking His presence and very gently summoning us to an attentive response. We are quite passive. We let it happen. "Let this little word represent to you God in all His fullness and nothing less than the fullness of God. Let nothing except God hold sway in your mind and heart" (C, chap. 4).

The subtle thing here is the effortlessness. We are so used to being very effortful. We are a people out to succeed, to accomplish, to do. It is hard for us to let go and let God do. And, after all, if *we* do, if we expend great effort, then when it is done we can pat ourselves on the back and salute ourselves for our great accomplishment. This prayer leaves no room for pride. We have but to let go and let it be done unto us according to His revealed Word. The temptation for us is to change the quiet mental repetition of the prayer word which simply prolongs a state of being present into an effortful repetition of an ejaculation and to use it energetically to knock out any thoughts or "distractions" that come along. This brings us to our third point.

> Three: Whenever in the course of the prayer we become aware of anything else, we simply gently return to the prayer word.

I want to underline the word *aware*. Unfortunately we are not able to turn off our minds and imaginations by the flick of a switch. Thoughts and images keep coming in a steady stream. "No sooner has a man turned toward God in love when through human frailty he finds himself distracted by the remembrance of some created thing or some daily care. But no matter. No harm done. For such a person quickly returns to deep recollection" (C, chap. 4).

In this prayer we go below the thoughts and images offered by the mind and imagination. But at times they will grab at our attention and try to draw it away from the restful Presence. This is so because these thoughts or images refer to something that has a hold on us, something we fear, or desire, or are in some other way intensely involved with. When we become *aware* of these thoughts, if we continue to dwell on them, we leave our prayer and become involved again in the tensions. But if, at the moment of *awareness*, we simply, gently return to our prayer word (thus implicitly renewing our act of presence in "faith-full" love), the thought or image with its attendant tension will be released and flow out of our lives. And we will come into a greater freedom and peace that will remain with us after our prayer is ended.

> Should some thought go on annoying you demanding to know what you are doing, answer with this one word alone. If your mind begins to intellectualize over the meaning and connotation of this little word, remind yourself that its value lies in its simplicity. Do this and I assure you these thoughts will vanish (C, chap. 7).

We can see how pure this prayer is. In active forms of prayer we use thoughts and images as sacraments and means of reaching out to God. In this prayer we go beyond them, we leave them behind, as we go to God

Himself abiding in our depths. It is a very pure act of faith. Perhaps in this prayer we will for the first time really act in pure faith. So often our faith is leaning on the concepts and images of faith. Here we go beyond them to the Object Himself of faith, leaving all the concepts and images behind.

We can see, too, how Christian this prayer is. For we very truly die to ourselves, our more superficial selves, the level of our thoughts, images, and feelings, in order to live to Christ, to enter into our Christ-being in the depths. We "die" to all our thoughts and imaginings, no matter how beautiful they may be or how useful they might seem. We leave them all behind, for we want immediate contact with God Himself, and not some thought, image, or vision of Him—only the faith experience of Himself. "You are to concern yourself with no creature, whether material or spiritual, nor with their situation or doings, whether good or ill. To put it briefly, during this work you must abandon them all" (C, chap. 5).

"By Their Fruits..."

There is another consequence of this transcending of thought and image. This prayer cannot be judged in itself. As it goes beyond thought, beyond image, there is nothing left by which to judge it. In active meditation, at the end of the prayer we can make some judgments. "I had some good thoughts, I felt some good affections, I had lots of distractions, and so forth." But all that is irrelevant to this prayer. If we have lots of thoughts—good, lots of tension is being released; if we have few thoughts—good, there was no need for them. The same for feelings, images, and the like. All these are purely accidental; they do not touch the essence of the prayer, which goes on in all its purity, whether these be present or not. There is nothing left by which to judge the prayer in itself. If we simply follow the three points, the prayer is always good, no matter what we think or feel.

There is, however, one way in which the goodness of this prayer is confirmed for us. Our Lord has said, "You can tell a tree by its fruit" (Matt. 7:20). If we are faithful to this form of prayer, making it a regular part of our day, we very quickly come to discern—and often others discern it even more quickly—the maturing in our lives of the fruits of the Spirit: love, joy, peace, patience, benignity, kindness, gentleness—all the fruits of the Spirit. I have experienced this in my own life and I have seen this again and again in the lives of others, some-times in a most remarkable way. What happens—the way the Spirit seems to bring this about—is that in this prayer we experience not only our oneness with God in

Christ, but also our oneness with all the rest of the Body of Christ, and indeed with the whole of creation, in God's creative love and sharing of being. Thus we begin, connaturally as it were, to experience the presence of God in all things, the presence of Christ in each person we meet. Moreover, we sense a oneness with them. From this flows a true compassion—a "feeling with." This contemplative prayer, far from removing us from others, makes us live more and more conscious of our oneness with them. Love, kindness, gentleness, patience grow. Joy and peace, too, in the pervasive presence of God's caring love in all. Not only does contemplative prayer help us to take possession of our real transcendent relationship with God in Christ, but also of our real relationship with each and every person in Christ.

May this simple form of prayer prove to be for you, and for those with whom you share it, a gentle, loving invitation from the Lord to a fuller, richer, deeper life in Him, a life marked by the fruits of the Holy Spirit.

CULTIVATING THE CENTERING PRAYER

THOMAS KEATING, OCSO

A practical method of contemplative prayer based on
The Cloud of Unknowing, developed by Father William
Meninger and called *centering prayer*, has been made
available by means of tapes, workshops sponsored by
the Religious Life Committee of the Conference of
Major Superiors of Men, and the increasing number of

retreats in different parts of the country designed to communicate this method. An introduction to the centering prayer by Father Basil Pennington appeared in the *Review for Religious* in September, 1976. His book on the same subject, *Daily We Touch Him*, was published by Doubleday in March, 1977. [Editor's Note: See the Resources section on pages 101–103 for an updated list of books on Centering Prayer.]

In any form of prayer, listening, waiting, and attending to God have an important place. This article explains centering prayer in relation to the kinds of thoughts that occur in the silence of listening and indicates how to cope with them. How to cope with unwanted thoughts is of crucial importance since it affects the quality of prayer, its refreshment, and the presence or absence of tension. The considerations proposed in this article in reference to the practice of centering prayer, therefore, may be applied, in a manner adapted to it, to one's own preferred form of prayer.

I.

Centering prayer is a renewal of the traditional prayer of the Church leading to contemplation. It is an attempt to present it in an up-to-date format and to put a certain order and method into it. This prayer is not meant to replace all other kinds of prayer. But it puts all the other kinds into a new perspective. It centers one's attention on God's presence within and moves on to discover His presence everywhere else. Thus it is not an end in itself, but a beginning. It is not to be done for the sake of an experience, but for the sake of its fruits in one's life. It also presupposes some dedication to God and some elementary spiritual formation.

Here is a parable that points to what is happening in this prayer.

There was a little fish who swam up to his mother one day and said: "Mummy, what is this ocean I hear so much about?"

She said to him, "You stupid little fish! It's all around you and in you. Just swim up onto the beach and lie there for a while and you'll find out."

Another time, there was a little bear who walked up to his mother one day and said: "Mummy, what is this air I hear so much about?"

She said to him, "You stupid little bear! It's all around you and in you. Just stick your head in a pail of water for a while, and you'll find out."

Finally, there was a certain beginner in the spiritual life who was having a hard time. One day he went up to his spiritual director and said: "What is this God I hear so much about?"

The spiritual director should not, of course, say to him, "You stupid little novice! He's all around you and in you." But he is supposed to be able to tell him what to do to discover and experience this reality.

Centering prayer is one way of doing this. By turning off the ordinary flow of thoughts, which reinforces one's habitual way of looking at the world, one's world begins to change. It is like turning a radio from long wave to short wave. You may be used to a long wave set and the stations it picks up, but if you want to hear stations from far away, you have to turn to the other wave length. In similar fashion, if you turn off your ordinary thought patterns, you enter into a new world of reality.

To do this systematically, take up a position that will enable you to sit still. Close your eyes. Half of the world disappears, because we think most of what we see. Then slow down the normal flow of thoughts by thinking just one thought. Choose a sacred word of one or two syllables that you feel comfortable with. "A one-syllable word such as 'God' or 'love' is best," says the author of *The Cloud*, "But choose one that is meaningful to you" (chap. 7). It will be the sign of your intention to open yourself interiorly to the mystery of God's enveloping presence. Keep thinking this sacred word. "This word will be your defense in conflict and in peace" (chap. 7). When you become aware that you are off on some other thought, gently return to this word. "Never strain your mind or imagination," warns the author of *The Cloud*, "for truly you will not succeed this way" (chap 4). As you go to a deeper level of reality, you begin to pick up vibrations that were there all the time but not perceived. This broadened perspective gives you a chance to know both yourself and God in a new way. However, as *The Cloud* says: "Your senses and faculties will be frustrated for lack of something to dwell on and they will chide you for doing nothing. But never mind. Go on with this *nothing*, moved only by your love for God.... Who do you suppose derides it as an emptiness? Our superficial self, of course. Certainly not our true self; no, our true self appreciates it as a fullness beyond measure. For in this darkness we experience an intuitive understanding of everything material and spiritual without giving special attention to anything in particular" (chap. 68).

Our ordinary thoughts are like boats sitting on a river, so closely packed together that we cannot see the river that is holding them up. We are normally aware of one object after another passing across the inner screen of consciousness: thoughts, memories, feelings, external objects. By slowing down that flow for a little while, space begins to appear between the boats. Up comes the reality on which they are floating.

The prayer of centering is a method of directing our attention from the boats to the river on which they are resting, from the particular to the general, from the concrete to the formless. At first you are preoccupied by the boats that are going by. You become interested to see what is on them. You must train yourself to let them all go by. If you catch yourself becoming interested in them, return to the sacred word you have chosen, which expresses the movement of your whole being toward God who is present within you.

A familiar gesture of devotion consists in placing the palms of the hands together with fingers pointing upward. It is meant to express the movement of our body and soul toward God. All our faculties are gathered together and pointed toward God by this gesture. That is what the sacred word is trying to say. It is a pointer. The word itself can become vague or disappear. It can be only an impulse of the will. But it points one's whole being to God.

II.

Various kinds of thoughts may come down the stream of consciousness when one starts to quiet one's mind. The appropriate response is a little different for each. The most obvious are the superficial thoughts that the imagination grinds out because of its natural propensity for perpetual motion. These should be treated like the weather which you just have to accept. The important thing is not to pay any attention to them. They are like the noise in the street which floats through the window of an apartment where two people are carrying on a conversation. Their attention is firmly directed to each other, but they cannot avoid hearing the noise. Sometimes they reach a point where they don't notice it at all. At other times the honking of horns may distract them momentarily. It would be useless to get in the elevator and go downstairs and tell the people on the street to shut up. You would have to discontinue the conversation, and you might not be able to take it up again where you left off. The only reasonable attitude is to put up with the noise and pay as little attention to it as possible. In this way you give as much of your undivided attention as circumstances allow to the person with whom you are conversing.

The second kind of thought occurs when you get interested in something that is happening in the street. A brawl breaks out and attracts your curiosity. This is the kind of thought that calls for some reaction. Here is where returning gently to the sacred word is a means of getting back to the general loving attention you are offering to God. It is important not to be annoyed with yourself if you get involved with these interesting thoughts. That would be a great mistake, because any annoyance or any curiosity that you give in to is another thought, and that takes you farther away from the interior silence which is the proximate goal of this prayer. Interior silence is always going to be relative.

It is important not to reflect on what is happening while doing centering prayer. You can do that later. While in this prayer, dedicate the time to interior silence.

III.

As we sink into deep peace and then silence, a third kind of thought may arise. Something in our nature—or maybe it is the devil—starts fishing. Brilliant intellectual or theological insights or what seem to be marvelous psychological breakthroughs, like tasty bait, are dangled in front of our minds and we think, "If only I can remember this fantastic insight!" But acquiescence to some beautiful or illuminating thought long enough to remember it afterwards will bring you out of the deep waters of silence. Any thought will bring you out. The author of *The Cloud* says, "I urge you to dismiss every clever or subtle thought no matter how holy or valuable. Cover it with a thick *cloud of forgetting* because in this life only love can touch God as He is in Himself, never knowledge" (chap. 8).

A very delicate but intimate kind of self-denial is necessary in this prayer. It is not just an experience of rest and refreshment—a sort of spiritual cocktail hour. It involves the denial of what we are most attached to, namely, our own thoughts and feelings—our very selves. As the author of *The Cloud* puts it: [This contemplative work] "is what leads you to a silence beyond thought and words and what makes your prayer simple and brief. And it is what teaches you to forsake and repudiate all that is false in the world. But even more, it is what teaches you to forsake and repudiate your very self according to the Gospel's demand: 'Let anyone who wishes to come after me deny himself, carry his cross, and follow me'" (*The Book of Privy Counseling*, chap. 11).

This kind of asceticism goes to the very roots of our attachment to our superficial egocentric selves and teaches us to let go. It is the most thorough kind of self-denial, but also a delightful kind. Self-denial does not have to be afflictive to be effective.

This is not the time to think about praying for yourself or somebody else. You can do that at another time. The author of *The Cloud* says, "One loving blind desire for God alone is more valuable in itself, more pleasing to God and to the saints, more beneficial to your own growth, and more helpful to your friends, both living and dead, than anything else you could do" (chap. 9).

The basic principle for handling thoughts in this prayer is this: whatever thought, feeling, or experience attracts your attention, always return to the sacred word. A thought can be anything you notice—inwardly or outwardly. Even if you should have an overwhelming experience of God, this is not the time to think about it.

IV.

As you quiet down and go deeper, you may come to a place that is outside time. Time is the measure of motion. With few or no successive thoughts, you may experience the time of prayer passing like the snap of your fingers. "It certainly did not seem like half an hour."

As you settle down to deep peace and inner freedom from all thoughts, a great desire to reflect on what is happening may arise. You may think, "At last I am getting some place."

Or, "This feeling of peace is just great."

Or, "If I could make a mental note of how I got here so that I can get back to it whenever I want!" These are good examples of the fourth kind of thought. The author of *The Cloud* has this advice: "Firmly reject all clear ideas, however pious or delightful" (chap. 9).

In deep tranquillity you are offered a choice between

reflecting on what is going on or letting go in faith. If you let go, you go to deeper silence. If you reflect, you come out and have to start over. There will be a lot of starting over.

The presence of God is like the atmosphere we breathe. You can have all you want of it as long as you do not try to take possession of it and hang on to it. Nothing is more delightful than the divine presence. For that very reason we want to carve out a piece of it and hide it in the closet for safekeeping. But that is like trying to grasp a handful of air. As soon as your fingers close over it, it is gone. The presence of God does not respond to greed. It has a different dynamism. It is totally available, but on condition that we freely accept it and do not try to possess it.

This prayer is communion with the Spirit of God who is charity, pure gift. The possessive instinct in us wants to hang on to what is good for dear life—and the tranquillity is so good and brings such a deep sense of security that the temptation to hang on is very great. But let it go. Accept each period of centering prayer as it comes, without asking for anything, having no expectations. In that way its fruits will grow faster. As it is explained in *The Cloud*, "Indeed the very heart of this work is nothing else than a naked intent toward God for His own sake. I call it 'naked intent' because it is utterly disinterested. In this work the perfect artisan does not seek personal gain or exemption from suffering. He desires only God and Him alone" (chap. 24).

We always want to possess. That is why it is so hard to let go—why we want to reflect on moments of deep peace or union in order to remember how we got there and thus how to get back. But charity is non-possessive. It gives all back to God as fast as it comes. It keeps nothing for itself.

The tendency to reflect is one of the hardest things to handle in deep prayer. We want to savor the moment of pure joy, pure experience, pure awareness. But if you can gradually train yourself to let the temptation to reflect go by, just like any thought, you will pass to a new level of freedom, a more refined joy.

We are accustomed to think we do not experience something until we express it in a thought. It is difficult to be childlike, to enjoy what is happening and forget it when it has passed—to savor the immediacy of reality. Reflection is one step back from experience. It is a photograph of reality. As soon as you start to reflect, the experience is over. Reflection on joy is an attempt to possess it. Then it is lost.

This method of prayer is a training in self-surrender. It teaches us by our own experience and mistakes not to be possessive, but to let go. If in this prayer you can get over the inveterate habit of reflecting on what is going on—have peace and not think about having peace—then you will have learned how to do it.

V.

There is a fifth kind of thought which arises in centering prayer. Any form of meditation or prayer that transcends thinking sets off the dynamic of interior purification. This dynamic is a kind of divine psycho-therapy. The experience facilitates the coming to consciousness of one's motivation and evil tendencies, and sometimes enables the organism to release deep rooted tension in the form of thoughts. Generally, thoughts which are the result of this process arise in the mind when one is most at peace, without one's knowing where they come from or why. They may introduce themselves with a certain force or even with an emotional charge. Once again, the best way to handle them is to return to the sacred word.

If you can once grasp the fact that thoughts are not only inevitable, but necessary as part of a process of healing and growth initiated by divine grace, you will be able to take a positive view of them. Instead of looking upon them with negative feelings as distractions, you see them in a broader perspective that includes both silence *and* thoughts—thoughts that you do not want or accept, but which, for the purpose of inward purification, are just as valuable as moments of profound tranquillity.

There is, finally, a sixth kind of thought, but this one is to be accepted and not disregarded. When in the seed-bed of deep interior silence, the mustard seed of divine charity has been sown by the Holy Spirit and begins to grow, it creates within what the author of *The Cloud* calls "a blind stirring of love." This awareness is the goal of centering prayer, the beginning of divine union. "For the work of perfect love which begins here on earth," says the author of *The Cloud*, "is the same as that love which is eternal life; they are both one" (chap. 20).

Elsewhere he adds: "*Stirring* does not refer to physical movement anymore than *rest* refers to stationary position. For when our work is authentic and mature it is entirely spiritual, far removed from movement or repose. Besides, *stirring* could actually be better expressed as a sudden transformation than a motion. In any case, you must forget all about time, place, and matter in this spiritual work" (chap. 59).

VI.

Take everything that happens during the periods of centering prayer peacefully and gratefully, without putting a judgment on anything, and just let the thoughts go by. It does not matter where they come from, as long as you let them go by. Don't worry about them. Don't fret about them. Don't judge the prayer on the basis of how many thoughts come. Simply follow the fundamental directive. When you are interested in a thought, either positively or negatively, return to the sacred word—and keep returning to it. This is fulfilling the Gospel precept to watch and pray. It is a waiting game to the "nth" degree. The author of *The Cloud* adds, "Do not imprudently strain yourself in this work. Rely more on joyful enthusiasm than on sheer brute force. For the more joyfully you work, the more humble and spiritual your contemplative work becomes, whereas when you morbidly drive yourself, the fruits will be gross and unnatural" (chap. 46).

All through the prayer of centering your mind will be in and out of deep silence—like a balloon floating in the air on a calm day. Just when it seems to be sinking and about to touch the earth, along comes a little zephyr from nowhere and up goes the balloon. So it is with our consciousness. You should pick up the sacred word at whatever level you find it—a simple impulse of your will may be sufficient. Then you can go back into silence without delay. If you get angry—"O, I wish my mind would keep still!"—then you get thrown out farther.

You must be non-judgmental about particular experiences of this prayer. The only way to judge it is by its long-range fruits—whether in daily life you enjoy greater awareness of the presence of God, greater peace, humility, and charity. Having come to deep silence, you see more clearly your capacity to relate to others at the deepest level—to pass beyond superficial appearances like social status, race, nationality, and personal characteristics. In this regard, the author of *The Cloud* observes, "The work of love not only heals the roots of sin, but nurtures practical goodness. When it is authentic, you will be sensitive to every need and respond with a generosity unspoiled by selfish intent" (chap. 12).

To know God in this way is to perceive a new dimension to all reality. The ripe fruit of this prayer is to bring back into the humdrum routine of ordinary life, not just the thought of God, but the constant awareness of His presence beyond any concept. *He Who is*—is the infinite, incomprehensible, ineffable One—is the God of faith. In this prayer we are asking, "Who are you, Lord?"—and waiting for the answer.

CONTEMPLATIVE PRAYER IN CHRISTIAN TRADITION

THOMAS KEATING, OCSO

In the Christian tradition a positive attitude towards contemplation characterized the teaching of the Church for the first fifteen centuries, while a negative attitude has prevailed with growing intensity from the sixteenth century onward. An overview of the history of contemplative prayer may prove helpful in order to understand how this change of attitude developed, as well as the situation in which the Church now finds herself in regard to religious experience.

I.

The word *contemplation* is an ambiguous term in our day, because over the centuries the word has acquired many meanings and connotations. To emphasize the experiential knowledge of God, the Greek Bible used the word *gnosis* to translate the Hebrew word *da'ath*, a much stronger term which implies possession of the thing known, an extremely intimate kind of knowledge involving the whole person, not just the mind (cf. Psalm 139:1–6).

St. Paul used the word *gnosis* in his epistles to refer to the knowledge of God proper to those who love Him. He constantly asked this intimate knowledge for his disciples and prayed for it as if it were an indispensable element for the complete development of Christian life.

The Greek Fathers, especially Clement of Alexandria, Origen, and Gregory of Nyssa, borrowed from the Neoplatonists the term *theoria*. This originally meant the intellectual vision of the truth which the Greek philosophers regarded as the supreme activity of the wise man. To this technical term the Fathers added the meaning of the Hebrew *da'ath*, that is, the kind of experiential knowledge that comes through love. It was with this expanded understanding of the term that *theoria* was translated into the Latin *contemplatio* and handed down to us by Christian tradition.

This tradition was well summed up by Gregory the Great at the end of the sixth century. He described contemplation as a knowledge of God that is impregnated with love. For Gregory, contemplation is the fruit of reflection of the word of God in Scripture and at the same time a gift of God. It is a *resting* in God. In this resting or stillness the mind and heart are not actively seeking Him, but are beginning to experience, to taste, what they have been seeking. This places them in a state of tranquillity and profound interior peace. This state is not the suspension of all action, but a mingling of a few simple acts to sustain one's attention to God with the loving experience of God's presence.

This meaning of contemplation as the knowledge of God based on the intimate and loving experience of His presence remained the same until the end of the Middle Ages. Ascetical disciplines were always directed toward contemplation as the proper goal of every spiritual practice.

The method of prayer proposed for lay persons and monastics alike was called *lectio divina*, literally *divine reading*, a practice that involved reading Scripture, or more exactly, listening to it. Monastics were taught to repeat the words of the sacred text with their lips so that their bodies entered into the process. They sought to cultivate through *lectio divina* the capacity to listen at ever deepening levels of inward attention. Prayer was their response to the God to whom they were listening in Scripture and giving praise in the liturgy.

The reflective part, the pondering upon the words of the sacred text, was called *meditatio*, meditation. The spontaneous movement of the will in response to these reflections was called *oratio*, or affective prayer. As these reflections and acts of will simplified, one moved on to a kind of resting in God, and that was what they meant by *contemplatio*, contemplation.

These three acts—discursive meditation, affective prayer, and contemplation—could all take place during the same period of prayer. They were interwoven one into the other. Like the angels ascending and descending on Jacob's ladder, one's attention was expected to go up and down the steps of the ladder of consciousness. Sometimes one would praise the Lord with one's lips, sometimes with one's thoughts, sometimes with acts of will and sometimes with one's silence, with the rapt attention of contemplation. Contemplation was regarded as the normal development of listening to the word of God. One's approach to God was not compartmentalized into discursive meditation, affective prayer, and mystical contemplation, as it came to be from the sixteenth century onwards. The term *mental prayer*, with its distinct categories, did not exist in Christian tradition prior to that time.

II.

Around the twelfth century a marked development in religious thought took place. The great schools of theology were founded. It was the birth of precise analysis in regard to concepts, division into genera and species, definitions and classifications. This growing capacity for analysis was a significant development of the human mind. Unfortunately, this passion for analysis in theology was later to be transferred to the life and practice of prayer and bring to an end the simple, spontaneous prayer of the Middle Ages based on *lectio divina* with its opening to contemplation. Meanwhile the spiritual masters of the twelfth century, like Bernard of Clairvaux, Hugh and Richard of St. Victor, and William of St. Thierry, were developing a theological understanding of prayer and contemplation. The thirteenth century saw methods of meditation based on their teaching popularized by the Franciscans.

During the fourteenth and fifteenth centuries events occurred with great consequences for Christendom. The Black Death and the Hundred Years' War decimated cities, towns, and religious communities, while nominalism and the Great Schism brought on a general decadence in morals and spirituality. A movement of renewal called *Devotio Moderna* arose in the Low Countries towards 1380 and spread to Italy, France and Spain in response to the widespread need for reform. In an age when institutions and structures of all kinds were crumbling, the movement of *Devotio Moderna* sought to use the moral powers issuing from prayer as a means of self-discipline. By the end of the fifteenth century methods of mental prayer properly so called were elaborated, becoming more and more complicated and systematized as time went on. But even while this proliferation of systemic methods of prayer was taking place, contemplation was still presented as the ultimate goal of spiritual practice.

As the sixteenth century progressed, mental prayer came to be divided into discursive meditation if thoughts predominated; affective prayer if the emphasis was on acts of the will; and contemplation if graces infused by God were predominant. Discursive meditation, affective prayer, and contemplation were no longer different acts found in a single period of prayer, but distinct forms of prayer, each with its own proper aim, method, and purpose.

This division of the on-going development of prayer into compartmentalized units entirely separated from one another helped to further the incorrect notion that contemplation is an extraordinary grace reserved to the very few. The possibility of prayer opening out into contemplation tended to be regarded as very unlikely. Contemplation did not fit into the approved categories and therefore was discouraged.

III.

At the same time that the living tradition of Christian spirituality was diminishing, the Renaissance came on the scene bringing new challenges for the spiritual life to contend with. No longer were the social milieu and religious institutions supportive of the individual. There was need to reconquer the world for Christ in the face of the pagan elements that were taking over Christendom. It was not surprising that new forms of prayer should appear that were almost entirely ordered to an apostolic ministry. Obviously the new emphasis on apostolic life, especially as it was instituted by Ignatius, required a transformation of the forms of spirituality hitherto transmitted by the monks and mendicants. It was Ignatius whose genius and contemplative experience led him to channel the living contemplative tradition, which was in danger of being lost, into a form appropriate to the new age.

The *Spiritual Exercises* of St. Ignatius, composed between 1522 and 1526, are extremely important, both in themselves and in the way that history treated them, in order to understand the present state of spirituality in the Roman Catholic Church. Three methods of prayer are proposed in the *Spiritual Exercises*. The discursive meditations prescribed for the first week are made according to the method of the three powers: memory, intellect, and will. The memory is to recall the point chosen beforehand as the subject of the meditation. The intellect is to reflect on the lessons one wants to get from that point. The will is to make resolutions based on that point in order to put the lessons into practice. Thus, one is led to conversion and reformation of life.

The word *contemplation* in the *Spiritual Exercises* has a meaning different from its traditional one. It consists in gazing upon concrete objects of the imagination: seeing, for example, the persons in the Gospel as if they were present, hearing what they are saying, relating and responding to their words and actions. This is the method of contemplation prescribed for the Second Week and is aimed at developing affective prayer.

The third method of prayer in the *Spiritual Exercises* is called application of the five senses. It consists of successively applying in spirit the five senses to the subject of the meditation. This method is designed to dispose beginners to infused contemplation and to develop the spiritual senses in those who are already advanced in prayer.

Thus Ignatius did not propose only one method of prayer. The tendency to reduce the *Spiritual Exercises* to a method of discursive meditation seems to stem from the Jesuits themselves. In 1574 Everard Mercurian, the Father General of the Jesuits, in a directive to the Spanish province of the Society, forbade the practice of affective prayer and the application of the five senses. This prohibition was repeated in 1578. Thus the spiritual life of a significant portion of the Society of Jesus was forcibly limited to a single method of prayer, namely, meditation according to the three powers. Moreover, the discursive character of this meditation continued to grow in importance throughout the Society during the course of the eighteenth and nineteenth centuries. Most manuals of spirituality until well into this century limited instruction to schemas of discursive meditation.

To comprehend the impact of the latter development on the Church's recent history, we should keep in mind the pervasive influence which the Jesuits exercised in the Church as the outstanding representatives of the Counter-Reformation. Many congregations of men and women that were founded in the following centuries adopted the *Constitutions* of the Society of Jesus. They received at the same time the spirituality taught and practiced by the Society. Hence, they also received the limitations imposed, not by Ignatius, but by his less enlightened successors.

Ignatius wished to provide a spiritual formation that was an appropriate antidote for the new secular and individualistic spirit of the Renaissance and a form of contemplative prayer adapted to the apostolic needs of his time. The *Spiritual Exercises* are designed to form contemplatives in action. Taking into account the immense influence of the Society for good, if its members had been allowed to follow the *Spiritual Exercises* according to Ignatius' original intent, or if they had given more prominence to its own contemplative spiritual masters like Fathers Lallemant, Surin, Grou, and de Caussade, the present state of spirituality among Roman Catholics might be quite different.

IV.

Other events occurred to increase the hesitation of Roman Catholic authorities towards contemplative prayer. One of these was the controversy regarding Quietism, a set of spiritual teachings condemned in 1687 as a species of false mysticism by Innocent XII. The condemned teachings were ingenious. They consisted in making once and for all an act of love for God by which you gave yourself entirely to Him with the intention never to recall the surrender. As long as you never withdrew the intention to belong to God, divine union was assured and no need for effort either in prayer or outside it was recognized. The important distinction between a one-time intention, however generous, and achieving it as a permanent disposition seems to have passed unnoticed.

A milder form of this doctrine flourished in France in the latter part of the seventeenth century and became known as semi-Quietism. Bishop Bossuet, chaplain to the court of Louis XIV, was one of the chief enemies of this attenuated form of Quietism and succeeded in having it condemned in France. How much he exaggerated the teaching is hard to reconstruct at this distance in time. In any case, the controversy brought traditional mysticism into greater disrepute. From then on, reading about mysticism was frowned upon in seminaries and religious communities. According to Henri Bremond in his book, *The Literary History of Religious Thought in France*, no mystical writing of any significance occurred during the next several hundred years. The mystical writers of the past were ignored. Even passages from John of the Cross were thought to be suggestive of

Quietism, thus forcing his editors to tone down or expunge certain statements lest they be misunderstood and condemned. The unexpurgated text of his writings only appeared in our own century, four hundred years after its composition.

A further set-back for Christian spirituality was the heresy of Jansenism, which gained momentum during the seventeenth century. Although it too was eventually condemned, it left behind a pervasive anti-human attitude that perdured throughout the nineteenth century and on into our own time. Jansenism strongly questioned the universality of Jesus' saving power as well as the intrinsic goodness of human nature. The pessimistic form of piety which it fostered spread with the emigrees from France at the time of the French Revolution to many English-speaking regions including Ireland and the United States. Since it is largely from French and Irish stock that priests and religious in this country have come, Jansenistic narrowness together with its distorted asceticism has deeply affected the psychological climate of our seminaries and religious orders. Priests and religious are still shaking off the last remains of the negative attitudes which they absorbed in the course of their ascetical formation.

Another unhealthy trend in the modern Church was the excessive emphasis on private devotions, apparitions, and private revelations. This led to the devaluation of the liturgy together with the communitarian values and sense of transcendent mystery which good liturgy engenders. The popular mind continued to regard contemplatives as saints, wonder workers, or at the very least, extraordinary people. The true nature of contemplation remained obscure and confused with phenomena such as levitation, the stigmata, and visions, which are strictly accidental to it.

During the nineteenth century there were many saints, but few spoke or wrote of contemplative prayer. There was a renewal of spirituality in Eastern Orthodoxy, but the main stream of Roman Catholic development seemed to be legalistic in character, with a kind of nostalgia for the Middle Ages and for political influence that the Church exercised at that time.

Abbot Cuthbert Butler sums up the generally accepted teaching during the eighteenth and nineteenth centuries in his book, *Western Mysticism.* "Except for very unusual vocations," he writes, "the normal prayer for everyone including contemplative monks and nuns, bishops, priests, and lay people, was systematic meditation following a fixed method, which could be one of four: the meditation according to the three powers as laid down in the *Spiritual Exercises of St. Ignatius,* the method of St. Alphonsus (which was a slight reworking of the *Exercises*), the method described by St. Francis de Sales in *An Introduction to the Devout Life,* or the method of St. Sulpice."

These are all methods of discursive meditation only. Contemplation was regarded as extraordinary and identified with extraordinary phenomena—in other words, something miraculous to be admired from a safe distance, but left alone as dangerous, full of pitfalls, and not something to which the ordinary Christian, priest, or religious should aspire.

The final nail that was hammered into the coffin of the traditional teaching was the obvious consequence that it would be against humility to aspire to contemplative prayer. Novices and seminarians were thus presented with a highly truncated view of the spiritual life, one that did not accord with either Scripture or tradition, nor with the normal experience of growth in prayer. If one attempts to persevere in discursive meditation after the Holy Spirit has called one beyond it, as the Spirit ordinarily does, one is bound to end in a state of utter frustration. It is normal for the mind to move through many reflections on the same theme to a single comprehensive view of the whole, and then to rest with a simple gaze upon the truth. As devout people moved spontaneously into this development in their prayer, they were up against this very negative attitude. They hesitated to go beyond discursive meditation because of the warnings they had been given about the dangers of contemplation. In the end they either gave up mental prayer altogether as something for which they were evidently unsuited, or through the mercy of God found some way of persevering in spite of what must have seemed like insurmountable obstacles.

In any case, the post-Reformation teaching opposed to contemplation was the direct opposite to the previous teaching of the Church. The genuine Christian tradition, taught uninterruptedly for the first fifteen centuries, is that contemplation is the normal evolution of a genuine spiritual life and hence open to all Christians. All these historical and cultural factors help to explain why the traditional spirituality of the Western church has gradually been lost in recent centuries, and why Vatican II had to address itself to the acute problem of spiritual renewal.

V.

The main reason that the contemplative dimension of prayer is receiving attention in recent years is two-fold. One is that historical and theological studies have rediscovered the integral teaching of John of the Cross and other great masters of the spiritual life. The other is the challenge coming from the East, especially since World War II. Methods of meditation similar to contemplative prayer in the Christian tradition have proliferated, produced good results, and received much publicity. It is important for us to appreciate the values that are present in the genuine teachings of the great religions of the world.[1] Since the spiritual traditions of the East possess a highly developed psychological wisdom, we need to know something about them in order to meet people where they are today. Many serious seekers of truth study the Eastern religions, take courses in them in college or graduate school and practice forms of meditation inspired and taught by Eastern masters.

The revival of mystical theology began with the publication of *The Degrees of the Spiritual Life* by the Abbe Saudreau in 1896. He based himself on the teaching of John of the Cross. Subsequent studies have confirmed the wisdom of his choice. In *The Living Flame of Love,* there is a long digression in which St. John speaks of the transition from sensible devotion to a truly spiritual relationship with God.[2] All who seek to give themselves completely to God, he says, will "very quickly" enter this transitional period which is the beginning of con-

---

[1] See *Declaration on the Relationship of the Church to Non-Christian Religions* (Vatican II).

[2] *Living Flame,* Stanza III, 26–59.

templative prayer. But how quick is "very quickly"? Is it a few months or a few weeks? He does not say. But the idea that one has to undergo years of superhuman trials, be walled-up behind convent walls, or kill one's self with various ascetical practices before one can aspire to contemplation, reflects the attitude of a Jansenistic worldview or, at the very least, is an inadequate presentation of the Christian tradition.

VI.

The Church finds herself at this moment in an embarrassing situation. There are many sincere people in our day anxious to learn contemplative prayer, and her official ministers are often unable to say anything about it with the kind of conviction that comes from experience. For the various historical reasons outlined above, the road to the full development of the gifts of the Holy Spirit leading to contemplative prayer has been generally disregarded in seminaries, religious life, and on the parish level. What is desperately needed is a widespread renewal of the traditional teaching and the actual experience of contemplation, especially among priests and ministers.

Unless theology and Scripture studies are integrated into a deep understanding of the Christian mystery, based on an ongoing experience of it, preaching and the other ministries are not going to impress anybody. Among the many challenges which the Church faces today, the greatest challenge—without which the others cannot be met—is the challenge of spiritual renewal.

FINDING GRACE AT THE CENTER

THOMAS E. CLARKE, SJ

One of the exercises of interiority which has come into favor in the past few years in the United States has been termed the *centering prayer*. Like other recent approaches to prayer, most of which have been influenced by Zen Buddhism, Transcendental Meditation, or other currents of eastern spirituality, it directs the focus of mind and spirit inward, toward the self, the center, the still-point. Non-discursive in character, these approaches yield not a new rational understanding so much as a certain still-ness, peace, joy, freedom, awareness.[1]

Such exercises may or may not constitute prayer. It is well known that some of them are being used for such worldly purposes as winning hockey games and earning a faster dollar. They become prayer when they are drawn into a faith-response to life. They will be more fruitful for the Christian in prayer to the degree that they are supported by Christian faith in its doctri-nal expression. The present article seeks to provide, for those Christians who are or may be attracted to such centering exercises, the support of understanding their own practice of them in the context of the mystery of grace. More specifically, our theme is *the center*, that is, the place of meeting of the human spirit and the divine Spirit, and, in that meeting, the place where the Christian at prayer meets the whole of reality, divine and human, persons and things, time and space, nature and history, evil and good.

Some years ago Georges Poulet brilliantly investigated the traditional symbol of God as the sphere whose cen-ter is every where and whose circumference is nowhere (*Deus est sphaera cuius centrum ubique, circumferentia*

---

[1] See Basil Pennington, "Centering Prayer," pp. 19–44, above.

nusquam).[2] The stimulating material offered by this study provides a starting point for the present reflection. As the point, the center of the circle or sphere, defines every point within the sphere and on its circumference, so God, in knowledge and creative power that are without limit, defines and begets the whole of reality. "The center is the father of the circle," wrote Plotinus. So God fathers the reality of the universe. He is the still-point of the turning world. The circumference for this still-point nowhere to be found symbolizes the limitlessness of God's presence to the reality He has begotten. The infinitesimal point—infinity of concentration—and the unlocatable circumference—infinity of extension: these contrasting facets of the symbol suggest the incomprehensibility of God's relationship to the world, at once infinitely beyond and infinitely within His creation, or, in Augustine's phrase, *intimius intimo meo, altius altissimo meo.*

The relationship expressed in the symbol is one of presence by creative knowledge and creative power, which in God are one. All the reality within the sphere, being born from God, is from Him, toward Him, in Him, who is always effecting it by His knowledge and knowing it in His effecting of it. As Poulet writes:

---

[2]Georges Poulet, *Les Metamorphoses du Cercle* (Paris, 1961).

The position occupied by the central point of the circle represents not only the unity and fixity of the divine duration, but the multiplicity of simultaneous relationships that it has with the peripheral and mobile duration of creatures. Eternity is not simply the pivot around which time turns; it is also the point at which, as the rays of the circle, the events of past and future converge and are united in the consciousness of God.[3]

Insofar as it is material, the universe is known and powered by God precisely in time and in space. He is therefore present simultaneously, as center and as circumference, to every point of time and likewise to every point of space. The creation, however, does not lose its character of successiveness and diffusion by being thus known and powered.

Especially since the Renaissance, Poulet notes, this symbol has been dynamically understood. There is at once a radiation of all created reality from the divine center and a return to that center. The origin of the universe is its destiny. Within a Christian perspective, this radiation-return imaging of creation finds its peak in Incarnation (and indwelling), where God's coming to us is identical with our going to Him. It is only in the mind that movement out from and back to the center are distinguished.

---

[3] *Ibid.*, p. vii.

There is more. Because each human being is created according to God's image, it verifies the maxim, to the degree of its likeness to God. So of the human spirit, the person, made in God's image, we may and must say that it is a sphere whose center is everywhere and whose circumference is nowhere. This means that all that we have said of God may be said of the human person. Wherever there is a human being, then, there is a sphere of knowledge and power possessed of a certain infinitude, capable of intensively and extensively unlimited relationships with the whole of creation, and with the Creator, the divine center, Himself.

"The soul is a kind of center," says Giordano Bruno. "It is," adds Poulet, "a center, not only, as the mystics believe, because God has in it His chosen abode, but because this place of divine dwelling is also the convergence of all cosmic phenomena."[4] This place, he goes on to say, can be *any* place. Wherever the soul situates itself in the universe becomes a center-point for viewing and relating to the relationship of God and the universe.

For us moderns, this kind of spiritual reflection, in which metaphysical and mathematical modes of abstraction are joined for the nourishment of the spirit, is at once attractive and yet somehow out of reach. We are children of subjectivity, and need to invest even traditional

---

[4] *Ibid.*, p. xxii.

symbols with the resonances of an experience of human life that is vastly different from that of ancient and medieval humans. Our journey to the center, and our abiding there, remains an enchanting symbol, but the language in which we describe it will be different from that of our ancestors.

When, as a modern Christian, I yield to the attraction of journeying to the center of my being, my faith tells me that this center is both my own human self, the image of God that I am, and the Self of God, the Holy Spirit, given precisely to be the selfing of myself, bestowed in order to give me (back) to myself by being given to me as the Self of Father and Son. Without a pantheistic identifying of Creator and creature, without denying that the self-gift of God is totally gift, grace, I as a Christian affirm (and as a praying Christian I act on the affirmation of) this unfathomable mystery of the Holy Spirit dwelling within my spirit, as the divine Self selfing my human self: and hence as transforming Center of my center.

This mystery means that my innate capacity as God's image to contain the whole of reality, created and uncreated, in knowledge and in power, and hence to be unlimited center and circumference of an infinite sphere, has been restored and transfigured by being drawn within the divine center and centering. When I make the journey to the Center, then, I am where I can touch and be present to all that is, including God Himself. Let me explore some of the facets of this presence.

First, when I am at the Center I am present to my own *personal history*. Physiologists and psychologists can tell me how the self that I am today is the self that I have become out of every instant of my human existence. From the particular night that I was conceived by parents who loved each other and so loved me into existence, I have been and become a self, a subject, a person, touched and shaped by a myriad of influences, all of which are present to me when I am present to myself, at the Center. The sickness at five weeks that almost ended my pilgrimage, the impact of losing my mother at nine, the successes and setbacks of childhood and adolescence, and all the rest, have been recorded in me in the way in which the rings of a tree are shaped by each year's sun and storms, or the way in which earth's tremors are recorded on a seismograph. To the degree that I am at the center of my self, the divine Self delivers into my hands, for sharing and for future 'selfing', this selfing history that is mine.

Similarly, at the Center I am present to myself in space, in my extension into the successive folds and layers of my humanity. From marrow to skin and hair, from deepest unconscious to sensate awareness, the

Spirit who knows and shapes me through and through offers me myself for stewarding and for simple cherishing. The wonderful reality that I am is most experienced as wonderful when I am at the Center. Here is where I can most fruitfully be in touch with my various gifts. This is the place, for example, where the fact that I know enough Greek to read the New Testament in the original, and enough Hebrew to be able to look up precious words in a dictionary, is gratefully drawn into the reality of my life with God. To the degree that I am at the Center, my ability to compose and to write, bestowed through the educative processes of many years, is met and enjoyed by me in an inner sanctuary, where it is cherished as ikon, not worshipped as idol.

The Center is the place, too, where I can most creatively meet the behavior, attitudes, options, awarenesses, and responses which constitute my moral, spiritual, and religious life. The 'consciousness examen' heals, reshapes, intensifies, to the degree that it takes place at the Center. It is here that the Artist, using no other clay than that which I bring from my earthly struggle to live humanly, patiently, refashions me in the image of Jesus Christ.

Because I am not a monad but a cell, the journey to the Center is the way that I walk in order to find other persons, other cells, other centers. The vistas opened up by this interpersonal aspect of centering prayer are immense. Saying something about this here will help, perhaps, to dissipate the objection that centering is an egocentric and narcissistic project. As love of myself is the base from which I can love others, so being at my own center, at this juncture of the divine Center and my own deepest self, means being at the heart of communion with other human beings. Who are they, and what is the import of my being with them at the Center?

They are those whom I name, in a special sense, my dear ones—my parents, brothers, family, Jesuit and other friends, more intimately known. What nourishment for the spirit there is, for example, in remembering how my father and mother were for one another and for me and my brothers in the days of long ago, or in holding communion with a dear one who happens to be on another continent.

Beyond this circle of intimates, there are all the persons who have, in however fleeting a fashion, touched my life in a personal way: the doctor who removed an abscess a few years ago, that strange science teacher of my high school days, the persons I have corresponded with without ever having met face to face. There are some famous people whom I have been privileged to meet in a more or less passing way: Dorothy Day (first when I was a high school student), Mother Teresa (about five years ago), Karl Rahner. And several times I have visited the grave of Pierre Teilhard de Chardin, who is buried in the cemetery of my old novitiate. All these help to comprise "those whom you have given me" (Jn. 17:11), and in some fashion I will, in the day of judgment, have to render an account for this accumulation of gifts. They, too, can be met throughout life at the Center.

Even beyond this wider circle of those whom I can name as fellow pilgrims, there are the four billion contemporaries who share the planet with me at this moment. I have seen some of their faces on the television screen, or brushed past them in airports, or sat next to them on buses or trains. All of us, however unequally, are nourished at the breasts of the same Mother Earth. We live together in statistical tables, within the bowels of the same computers. Some of them harvest the grain and the grapes of my daily Eucharist. Quite starkly, some of them die, or are doomed to an early death, because the dark principalities and powers of contemporary economic and political life provide me with necessities and even superfluities at the price of their very survival. Whoever they are, and whatever may be the tragic aspects of their relationship to me, it is at the Center that I am in closest touch with them.

Then there is the caravan of humanity of preceding ages. Because the Center is a point simultaneously present to all instants of human duration, I can meet there the celebrated and the anonymous, the saints and the sinners, stretching back to humanity's origins. Somewhere, in the late tenth century for example, somewhere in northern Europe, a man and woman came together in some beautiful or dismal or violent way, and their joining formed one link in the chain of life which eventually came to me. Who are they, and what is my kinship with them? It is at the Center that I know, insofar as I can know.

Next, there is the great cloud of witnesses, the saints, celebrated or not, who by their deeper presence to the Center are present to every pilgrim center, including mine. I bear the name of a few of them, and have special links with others by the fact that I share a special ethnic, national, religious heritage, or because at some point of my journey God brought them across my path. Worthy of special marvel is the way in which one woman, Mary of Nazareth, came to be part of this community of the Center, for me and for millions of others.

It need hardly be said that the human presence which, more than any other, I find at the Center, is Jesus Himself—and first of all in His own pilgrim story. However little of that history I have access to by ordinary channels, there is a real sense in which I can appropriate every detail of it when I am at the Center.

This is true of all human relationships. Even before there is an explicit knowledge of the life-history of a loved one, we take hold of it by taking hold of the loved one, for they carry their history within them as we carry ours. So what takes place at the Center is the mingling and sharing of these two personal histories, Jesus' and mine. His being now the risen Lord, present in the hiddenness of His glory, introduces no dualism into my communion with Him at the Center. For precisely because we are at the central point simultaneously present to all duration, the Jesus of history and the Christ of faith are one in this personal encounter.

And, finally, through Jesus, I am at the Center present to God as Father, Son, Spirit. It is interesting that the medieval symbol of the infinite sphere received a trinitarian interpretation, in which Son and Spirit were imaged as going forth from the Father, as ripples from a generating point. There are undoubtedly various ways of conceiving theologically how the triune God is met at the Center. A christocentric view such as that of Emile Mersch would speak of a certain mediation of the humanity of the Word, so that it is through the Son, and, indeed, through His body which is the Church, that we have our relationship with the Father and the Spirit. A different theology would make the Spirit, not the Son, the point of entry, so to speak, into trinitarian life. Such theological refinements make little difference, perhaps, especially to the degree that presence to the Trinity at the Center takes place without the mediation of intellectual or imaginative forms. The point to be made is that the Center is where I find the life of my action, the exemplar of my witness, the unfathomable source of my very existence: Spirit, Son, Father.

We have still not exhausted the possibilities of finding the whole of reality at the Center. There is no space for a detailed account of the other encounters which can take place; but a summary of some of these may suggest what riches are available for one who knows how to journey to the Center.

1. The public history of humanity, the unfolding of age upon age, the rise and fall of cultures and civilizations. What perspectives can be gained on one's personal life, and on the struggles of the Church and of humanity today, by being in touch with the flow of human history at the center of our being!

2. The riches of diverse cultures, the arts and sciences and techniques as they have been developed in human history, from the striking of the first flint to the development of the most sophisticated computer, from scratchings on the walls of prehistoric caves to the latest Picasso. In our

museums we cherish each tiny witness to the glories of creation as they are crystallized in the story of human endeavors. Yet the treasures of the past, the heritage of history, is fully available for our creation of a human future only when they are brought to the deepest heart of our humanity, to the Center. In fact, only the habit of journeying to the Center can keep us from desecrating our heritage. Compare, for example, the availability of the music of Bach and Beethoven for even the wealthiest and most cultured groups in, say, the seventeenth century, with their instant availability for millions today. We should not too quickly assume that this wider diffusion is proportionately enriching. The very facility of access brings a danger of trivialization, as when, for example, Bach and Beethoven become background music for work or entertainment, or the Mona Lisa is commercially exploited. Our artistic heritage is best cherished, it seems to me, when it is carried with us in our journey to the Center.

3. The theological understanding of our faith, and of life in the light of faith. It is the deficiency of much theologizing, both professional and popular, that it is conducted at the more superficial levels of human discourse. Bringing theology to the center is like dipping a fabric in a liquid which restores and transfigures its inherent beauty. This

is the place where the great doctors of the Church carried on their pondering of the mystery. Only to the degree that theology takes place in the stillness of the Center will it be capable of nourishing the Church.

4. Liturgical celebration. A few decades ago, Jacques Maritain and others engaged in a lively debate on liturgy and contemplation. This concern needs to be perennial. Being at the center in liturgical celebration does not mean disengagement of sense and sensibility from the ritual action. On the contrary, the more one is at the still-point, the more he or she is capable of deep participation and communion with fellow worshippers. The journey inward takes place through interiorization, not through departure.

At this point there is need to note that, for purposes of analysis, I have been bracketing a most basic aspect of human life: sin and liberation from sin. The journey to the Center, however, takes place not within paradise but within a world of darkness and light, death and life, a world in which—so great is the mystery—God struggles with hostile forces and conquers them. While it is not possible to develop this aspect of our theme, it is clear how much it will affect the journey to the Center and what happens there. Grace and sin are correlatives, and the deeper our experience of the divine Center the deeper will be our experience of the evil of the world.

One specific corollary of this needs to be mentioned, in view of current concerns regarding justice, peace, and poverty. It would be a distortion of the meaning of this symbol of centering to conceive that movement to the Center brings with it, or even is compatible with, a disengagement from the human struggle for peace, justice, and other embattled public values. The quality and intensity of contemplation is in direct, not in inverse, proportion to the quality and intensity of our action on behalf of justice and peace, and vice versa. We are far enough into the polarities of the Church's engagement in today's struggle for human dignity to know that refusal or inability to journey to the Center is, however well-intentioned may be engagement in social ministries, a betrayal of the brother or sister. The opposite is also true: apparent journeys to the Center, which yield no fruit of compassion and justice, are thereby revealed to be eccentric wanderings and sham, the kind denounced by Amos and Isaiah and by Jesus Himself.

With this said, it is time to leave these more theoretical considerations and to speak of the way in which the journey to the Center may take place in prayer. I would like here to summarize what I have been saying. I have been proposing that the center of our human existence is the point at which our personhood, created in God's image and so radically capable of encompassing all reality, is intimately joined to God Himself, particularly as indwelling Spirit, and so transfigured in its character and capability of being a sphere whose center is everywhere and whose circumference is nowhere. Secondly, I have said that this presence at the Center is not a removal from the basic struggle of earthly life, from the conflict between the powers of light and of darkness, but rather a more intense engagement in that struggle, and a healing for this deeper engagement of the sinful person that I am. And thirdly, I have tried to illustrate how by appropriate presence at this Center we are in deepest touch with the whole of reality, created and divine.

Now I ask: How does one journey to the Center, and how does one behave there? This question concerns prayer, approaches to prayer, methods of prayer. My first and general response is that one journeys by walking, that there are different roads for different persons, and that the same person at different times will be drawn to walk by different roads.

The road of *darkness* is the one which is followed in the centering prayer to which I referred at the beginning of this essay. It will normally make use of a prayer word, preferably a single word, repeated or silently held in a kind of non-saying, with a frequency determined by the goal of leading one to silent presence at the Center. Such a method has much in common with the central image of *The Cloud of Unknowing,* where the person praying is situated between the cloud of forgetting (of creatures) below, and the cloud of unknowing (of the Creator) above, with a simple presence of the heart. Though the image is somewhat different, the prayer of centering has basically the same character. A certain silence and a certain darkness is the modality of presence at the Center. God is not overtly addressed or listened to or felt. And the same is true of the reality of creation. If, for example, I have entered into this exercise after worrying about a friend who is sick, or recalling an experience of childhood for which I am grateful, or focusing on a facet of contemporary life which is part of my apostolic concern, what is here characteristic is that *I let them go.* I do not think of them or image them in any way. If, especially out of anxiety, they emerge in overt presence, I am quietly aware of this fact, but then, just as quietly, let go of them again. The wonder and paradox is that they thus become, if anything, more deeply present to me, because they have been "lost" in the meeting of my center with the Center, who likewise, in this form of prayer, is not objectively attended to. This is, perhaps, all that needs to be said and can be said by way of describing this first, and perhaps most fruitful, way of journeying to the Center.

One final word may indicate how there is question here not just of particular exercises of prayer carried out at specified moments, in the interstices of life, as it were. The traditional distinction of formal and virtual (or habitual) prayer is operative here. The hope is that special practices of centering will foster facility, and that a *quality* may emerge and grow, by which each experience of each day takes place at the Center. We have all met persons for whom this seems to be true to a marvelous degree. And we have met, in prayer, Jesus Christ, through whom we have come to know that this is the modality of existence eternally shared by Father, Son, and Spirit. The insight of the tradition that *any place* can be a center is founded, ultimately, on the conviction of faith that the Center who imaged us forth is both everywhere and nowhere.

Focus on
Centering Prayer

In the center of your being lives God: Father, Son, and Spirit. Centering prayer allows you to experience His presence and be touched and transformed by Him.

Simply sit, relaxed and quiet, enjoying your own inner calm and silence. For a few moments, listen to His presence and allow yourself to be touched by it.

After a time, perhaps a single word will come: *Jesus, Lord, Love,* or any word that captures your response to His inner presence. Place into this word all your faith, your love, as you enter more and more deeply into Him. Slowly and effortlessly, repeat your word. Allow it to lead you more and more deeply into God's presence at the center of your being, where you are in God and God in you. Surrender to His re-freshment and re-creation.

Center all your attention and desire on Him, leaving your faculties at peace, allowing Him to draw you into His perfect prayer of adoration, love, and praise. Let it happen. Whenever you become aware of any thoughts or images, simply return to your word.

In coming out of prayer, move slowly to silent awareness and then a conscious interior prayer, such as the *Our Father,* savoring the words and meaning, entering into them.

The centering prayer may be used once or twice daily for twenty minutes or more.

If you are faithful to it, you will soon discern in your life the maturing of the fruits of the *Spirit*: love, joy, peace, patience, gentleness, and kindness.

You shall be truly abiding in Him and He in you.

ℛESOURCES

Books

Arico, Carl J. *A Taste of Silence: Centering Prayer and the Contemplative Journey* (New York: Continuum, 1999).

Bourgeault, Cynthia. *Centering Prayer and Inner Awakening* (Cambridge, MA: Cowley Publications, 2004).

Keating, Thomas. *Awakenings* (New York: Crossroad, 1990).

———. *The Better Part: Stages of Contemplative Living* (New York: Continuum, 2000).

———. *The Heart of the World: An Introduction to Contemplative Christianity,* as told to John Osborne (New York: Continuum, 1999).

———. *The Human Condition: Contemplation and Transformation* (New York: Paulist Press, 1999).

——— *Intimacy with God* (New York: Crossroad, 1994).

———. *Invitation to Love: The Way of Christian Contemplation* (Rockport, Mass.: Element, 1992).

———. *Journey to the Center: A Lenten Passage* (New York: Crossroad, 1999).

———. *Open Mind, Open Heart: The Contemplative Dimension of the Gospel* (Rockport, Mass.: Element, 1992).

———. *Reawakenings* (New York: Crossroad, 1992).

Meninger, William A. *The Loving Search for God: Contemplative Prayer and The Cloud of Unknowing* (New York: Continuum, 1994).

Pennington, M. Basil. *Awake in the Spirit: A Personal Handbook on Prayer* (New York: Crossroad, 1992).

————. *Call to the Center: The Gospel's Invitation to Deeper Prayer* (Hyde Park, N.Y.: New City Press, 1995).

————. *Centered Living: The Way of Centering Prayer* (Liguori, Mo.: Liguori, 1999).

————. *Centering Prayer: Renewing an Ancient Christian Prayer Form* (Garden City, N.Y.: Image Books, 1982).

————. *Daily We Touch Him: Practical Religious Experiences* (Kansas City: Sheed & Ward, 1997).

————. *An Invitation to Centering Prayer* (Liguori, Mo.: Liguori, 2001).

————. *Lectio Divina: Renewing the Ancient Practice of Praying the Scriptures* (New York: Crossroad, 1998).

————. *A Place Apart: Monastic Prayer and Practice for Everyone* (Liguori, Mo.: Liguori/Triumph, 1998).

————. *Psalms: A Spiritual Commentary* (Woodstock, Vt.: SkyLight Paths, 2006).

————. *The Song of Songs: A Spiritual Commentary* (Woodstock, Vt.: SkyLight Paths, 2004).

Reininger, Gustave, ed. *Centering Prayer in Daily Life and Ministry* (New York: Continuum, 1998).

————. *The Diversity of Centering Prayer* (New York: Continuum, 1999).

Audiotape Cassettes

Arico, Carl. *The Power of Silence* (3 tapes).

Keating, Thomas. *Centering Prayer* (3 tapes).

————. *Divine Therapy* (4 tapes).

————. *The Gift of Contemplation and the Spiritual Journey* (6 tapes).

————. *Journey to Contemplation* (8 tapes).

————. *Spirituality of Everyday Life* (5 tapes).

Mrozowskl, Mary. *Beyond Centering Prayer* (6 tapes).

Pennington, M. Basil. *Being Contemplative.*

————. *Contemplation in Context.*

————. *The Experience of God.*

————. *Gratefully Ourselves: True Self/False Self.*

Videotape Cassettes

Keating, Thomas. *The Contemplative Journey,* vols. 1 and 2 (24 tapes with study guide).

Pennington, M. Basil. *A Centering Prayer Retreat* (2 tapes).

————. *Contemplation for Everyone.*

————. *Nurturing Our Prayer.*

————. *Our Way to Happiness.*

————. *How to Center Your Life* (4 conferences).

————. *A Matter of Love* (4 conferences).

————. *Opening the Contemplative Dimension.*

About the Authors

M. Basil Pennington, ocso, was a monk for more than fifty years. He wrote many modern spiritual classics, including *Psalms: A Spiritual Commentary* (SkyLight Paths), and *Centering Prayer*.

Thomas Keating, ocso, is a monk, priest, and former abbot who currently lives at St. Benedict's Monastery in Snowmass, Colorado. His books include *Open Mind, Open Heart; Intimacy with God;* and many others.

Thomas F. Clarke, sj, is a well-known Jesuit writer and spiritual father. He now resides at Bethany Retreat Center in Highland Mills, New York.

AVAILABLE FROM BETTER BOOKSTORES.
TRY YOUR BOOKSTORE FIRST.

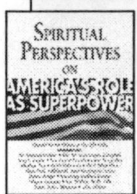

Global Spiritual Perspectives

Spiritual Perspectives on America's Role as Superpower
by the Editors at SkyLight Paths
Are we the world's good neighbor or a global bully? From a spiritual perspective, what are America's responsibilities as the only remaining superpower? Contributors:
Dr. Beatrice Bruteau • Dr. Joan Brown Campbell • Tony Campolo • Rev. Forrest Church • Lama Surya Das • Matthew Fox • Kabir Helminski • Thich Nhat Hanh • Eboo Patel • Abbot M. Basil Pennington, ocso • Dennis Prager • Rosemary Radford Ruether • Wayne Teasdale • Rev. William McD. Tully • Rabbi Arthur Waskow • John Wilson
5½ x 8½, 256 pp, Quality PB, 978-1-893361-81-2 **$16.95**

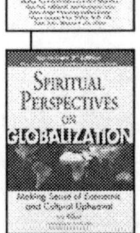

Spiritual Perspectives on Globalization, 2nd Edition
Making Sense of Economic and Cultural Upheaval
by Ira Rifkin; Foreword by Dr. David Little, Harvard Divinity School
What is globalization? Surveys the religious landscape. Includes a new Discussion Guide designed for group use.
5½ x 8½, 256 pp, Quality PB, 978-1-59473-045-0 **$16.99**

Hinduism / Vedanta

The Four Yogas
A Guide to the Spiritual Paths of Action, Devotion, Meditation and Knowledge
by Swami Adiswarananda 6 x 9, 320 pp, HC, 978-1-59473-143-3 **$29.99**

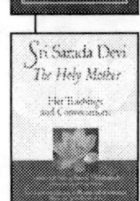

Meditation & Its Practices
A Definitive Guide to Techniques and Traditions of Meditation in Yoga and Vedanta
by Swami Adiswarananda 6 x 9, 504 pp, Quality PB, 978-1-59473-105-1 **$19.99**

The Spiritual Quest and the Way of Yoga: The Goal, the Journey and the Milestones
by Swami Adiswarananda 6 x 9, 288 pp, HC, 978-1-59473-113-6 **$29.99**

Sri Ramakrishna, the Face of Silence
by Swami Nikhilananda and Dhan Gopal Mukerji
Edited with an Introduction by Swami Adiswarananda; Foreword by Dhan Gopal Mukerji II
Classic biographies present the life and thought of Sri Ramakrishna.
6 x 9, 352 pp, HC, 978-1-59473-115-0 **$29.99**

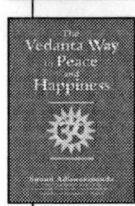

Sri Sarada Devi, The Holy Mother
Her Teachings and Conversations
Translated with Notes by Swami Nikhilananda; Edited with an Introduction by Swami Adiswarananda
6 x 9, 288 pp, HC, 978-1-59473-070-2 **$29.99**

The Vedanta Way to Peace and Happiness by Swami Adiswarananda
6 x 9, 240 pp, HC, 978-1-59473-034-4 **$29.99**

Vivekananda, World Teacher: His Teachings on the Spiritual Unity of Humankind
Edited and with an Introduction by Swami Adiswarananda
6 x 9, 272 pp, Quality PB, 978-1-59473-210-2 **$21.99**

Sikhism

The First Sikh Spiritual Master
Timeless Wisdom from the Life and Teachings of Guru Nanak by Harish Dhillon
Tells the story of a unique spiritual leader who showed a gentle, peaceful path to God-realization while highlighting Guru Nanak's quest for tolerance and compassion. 6 x 9, 192 pp, Quality PB, 978-1-59473-209-6 **$16.99**

Or phone, fax, mail or e-mail to: SKYLIGHT PATHS Publishing
Sunset Farm Offices, Route 4 • P.O. Box 237 • Woodstock, Vermont 05091
Tel: (802) 457-4000 • Fax: (802) 457-4004 • www.skylightpaths.com
Credit card orders: (800) 962-4544 (8:30AM–5:30PM ET Monday–Friday)
Generous discounts on quantity orders. SATISFACTION GUARANTEED. Prices subject to change.

Children's Spiritual Biography

MULTICULTURAL, NONDENOMINATIONAL, NONSECTARIAN

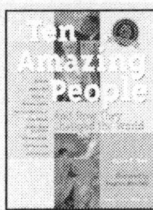

Ten Amazing People
And How They Changed the World
by Maura D. Shaw; Foreword by Dr. Robert Coles
Full-color illus. by Stephen Marchesi

(For ages 7 & up)

Black Elk • Dorothy Day • Malcolm X • Mahatma Gandhi • Martin Luther King, Jr. • Mother Teresa • Janusz Korczak • Desmond Tutu • Thich Nhat Hanh • Albert Schweitzer

This vivid, inspirational and authoritative book will open new possibilities for children by telling the stories of how ten of the past century's greatest leaders changed the world in important ways.

8½ x 11, 48 pp, HC, Full-color illus., 978-1-893361-47-8 **$17.95**
For ages 7 & up

Spiritual Biographies for Young People—For ages 7 and up

   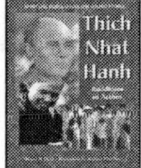

Black Elk: Native American Man of Spirit
by Maura D. Shaw; Full-color illus. by Stephen Marchesi
Through historically accurate illustrations and photos, inspiring age-appropriate activities and Black Elk's own words, this colorful biography introduces children to a remarkable person who ensured that the traditions and beliefs of his people would not be forgotten.
6¼ x 8¼, 32 pp, HC, Full-color and b/w illus., 970-1-59473-043-6 **$12.99**

Dorothy Day: A Catholic Life of Action
by Maura D. Shaw; Full-color illus. by Stephen Marchesi
Introduces children to one of the most inspiring women of the twentieth century, a down-to-earth spiritual leader who saw the presence of God in every person she met. Includes practical activities, a timeline and a list of important words to know.
6¼ x 8¼, 32 pp, HC, Full-color illus., 978-1-59473-011-5 **$12.99**

Gandhi: India's Great Soul
by Maura D. Shaw; Full-color illus. by Stephen Marchesi
There are a number of biographies of Gandhi written for young readers, but this is the only one that balances a simple text with illustrations, photographs, and activities that encourage children and adults to talk about how to make changes happen without violence. Introduces children to important concepts of freedom, equality and justice among people of all backgrounds and religions.
6¼ x 8¼, 32 pp, HC, Full-color illus., 978-1-893361-91-1 **$12.95**

Thich Nhat Hanh: Buddhism in Action
by Maura D. Shaw; Full-color illus. by Stephen Marchesi
Warm illustrations, photos, age-appropriate activities and Thich Nhat Hanh's own poems introduce a great man to children in a way they can understand and enjoy. Includes a list of important Buddhist words to know.
6¼ x 8¼, 32 pp, HC, Full-color illus., 978-1-893361-87-4 **$12.95**

Children's Spirituality—Board Books

Adam and Eve's New Day (A Board Book)
by Sandy Eisenberg Sasso; Full-color illus. by Joani Keller Rothenberg
A lesson in hope for every child who has worried about what comes next. Abridged from *Adam and Eve's First Sunset.*
5 x 5, 24 pp, Full-color illus., Board Book, 978-1-59473-205-8 **$7.99** *For ages 0–4*

How Did the Animals Help God? (A Board Book)
by Nancy Sohn Swartz; Full-color illus. by Melanie Hall
Abridged from *In Our Image*, God asks all of nature to offer gifts to humankind—with a promise that they will care for creation in return.
5 x 5, 24 pp, Board Book, Full-color illus., 978-1-59473-044-3 **$7.99** *For ages 0–4*

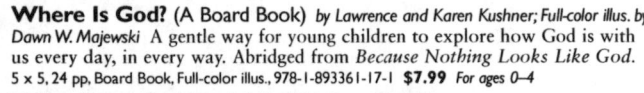

Where Is God? (A Board Book) *by Lawrence and Karen Kushner; Full-color illus. by Dawn W. Majewski* A gentle way for young children to explore how God is with us every day, in every way. Abridged from *Because Nothing Looks Like God.*
5 x 5, 24 pp, Board Book, Full-color illus., 978-1-893361-17-1 **$7.99** *For ages 0–4*

What Does God Look Like? (A Board Book)
by Lawrence and Karen Kushner; Full-color illus. by Dawn W. Majewski
A simple way for young children to explore the ways that we "see" God. Abridged from *Because Nothing Looks Like God.*
5 x 5, 24 pp, Board Book, Full-color illus., 978-1-893361-23-2 **$7.95** *For ages 0–4*

How Does God Make Things Happen? (A Board Book)
by Lawrence and Karen Kushner; Full-color illus. by Dawn W. Majewski
A charming invitation for young children to explore how God makes things happen in our world. Abridged from *Because Nothing Looks Like God.*
5 x 5, 24 pp, Board Book, Full-color illus., 978-1-893361-24-9 **$7.95** *For ages 0–4*

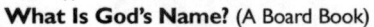

What Is God's Name? (A Board Book)
by Sandy Eisenberg Sasso; Full-color illus. by Phoebe Stone
Everyone and everything in the world has a name. What is God's name? Abridged from the award-winning *In God's Name.*
5 x 5, 24 pp, Board Book, Full-color illus., 978-1-893361-10-2 **$7.99** *For ages 0–4*

What You Will See Inside ...

This important new series of books, each with many full-color photos, is designed to show children ages 6 and up the Who, What, When, Where, Why and How of traditional houses of worship, liturgical celebrations, and rituals of different world faiths, empowering them to respect and understand their own religious traditions—and those of their friends and neighbors.

What You Will See Inside a Catholic Church
by Reverend Michael Keane; Foreword by Robert J. Keeley, EdD
Full-color photos by Aaron Pepis
8½ x 10½, 32 pp, Full-color photos, HC, 978-1-893361-54-6 **$17.95**

Also available in Spanish: **Lo que se puede ver dentro de una iglesia católica**
8½ x 10½, 32 pp, Full-color photos, HC, 978-1-893361-66-9 **$16.95**

What You Will See Inside a Hindu Temple
by Dr. Mahendra Jani and Dr. Vandana Jani; Full-color photos by Neirah Bhargava and Vijay Dave
8½ x 10½, 32 pp, Full-color photos, HC, 978-1-59473-116-7 **$17.99**

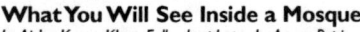

What You Will See Inside a Mosque
by Aisha Karen Khan; Full-color photos by Aaron Pepis
8½ x 10½, 32 pp, Full-color photos, HC, 978-1-893361-60-7 **$16.95**

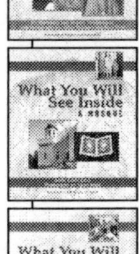

What You Will See Inside a Synagogue
by Rabbi Lawrence A. Hoffman and Dr. Ron Wolfson; Full-color photos by Bill Aron
8½ x 10½, 32 pp, Full-color photos, HC, 978-1-59473-012-2 **$17.99**

Children's Spirituality

ENDORSED BY CATHOLIC, PROTESTANT, JEWISH, AND BUDDHIST RELIGIOUS LEADERS

Adam and Eve's First Sunset: God's New Day
by Sandy Eisenberg Sasso; Full-color illus. by Joani Keller Rothenberg
9 × 12, 32 pp, Full-color illus., HC, 978-1-58023-177-0 **$17.95** *For ages 4 & up (a Jewish Lights book)*

Because Nothing Looks Like God
by Lawrence and Karen Kushner; Full-color illus. by Dawn W. Majewski
Real-life examples of happiness and sadness introduce children to the possibilities of spiritual life. 11 × 8½, 32 pp, HC, Full-color illus., 978-1-58023-092-6 **$16.95**
For ages 4 & up (a Jewish Lights book)

Also available: **Teacher's Guide,** 8½ × 11, 22 pp, PB, 978-1-58023-140-4 **$6.95** *For ages 5–8*

Becoming Me: A Story of Creation
by Martin Boroson; Full-color illus. by Christopher Gilvan-Cartwright
Told in the personal "voice" of the Creator, a story about creation and relationship
that is about each one of us.
8 × 10, 32 pp, Full-color illus., HC, 978-1-893361-11-9 **$16.95** *For ages 4 & up*

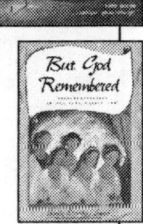

But God Remembered: Stories of Women from Creation to the
Promised Land *by Sandy Eisenberg Sasso; Full-color illus. by Bethanne Andersen*
A fascinating collection of four different stories of women briefly mentioned in bib-
lical tradition and religious texts. 9 × 12, 32 pp, HC, Full-color illus., 978-1-879045-43-9 **$16.95**
For ages 8 & up (a Jewish Lights book)

Cain & Abel: Finding the Fruits of Peace
by Sandy Eisenberg Sasso; Full-color illus. by Joani Keller Rothenberg
A sensitive recasting of the ancient tale shows we have the power to deal with anger
in positive ways. "Editor's Choice"—American Library Association's *Booklist*
9 × 12, 32 pp, HC, Full-color illus., 978 1 58023-123-7 **$16.95** *For ages 5 & up (a Jewish Lights book)*

Does God Hear My Prayer?
by August Gold; Full-color photos by Diane Hardy Waller
Introduces preschoolers and young readers to prayer and how it helps them express
their own emotions. 10 × 8½, 32 pp, Quality PB, Full-color photo illus., 978-1-59473-102-0 **$8.99**

The 11th Commandment: Wisdom from Our Children *by The Children of America*
"If there were an Eleventh Commandment, what would it be?" Children of many
religious denominations across America answer this question—in their own
drawings and words. "A rare book of spiritual celebration for all people, of all
ages, for all time." —*Bookviews*
8 × 10, 48 pp, HC, Full-color illus., 978-1-879045-46-0 **$16.95** *For all ages (a Jewish Lights book)*

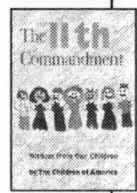

For Heaven's Sake *by Sandy Eisenberg Sasso; Full-color illus. by Kathryn Kunz Finney*
Everyone talked about heaven: "Thank heavens." "Heaven forbid." "For heav-
en's sake, Isaiah." But no one would say what heaven was or how to find it. So
Isaiah decides to find out, by seeking answers from many different people.
9 × 12, 32 pp, HC, Full-color illus., 978-1-58023-054-4 **$16.95** *For ages 4 & up (a Jewish Lights book)*

God in Between *by Sandy Eisenberg Sasso; Full-color illus. by Sally Sweetland*
A magical, mythical tale that teaches that God can be found where we are.
9 × 12, 32 pp, HC, Full-color illus., 978-1-879045-86-5 **$16.95** *For ages 4 & up (a Jewish Lights book)*

God's Paintbrush: Special 10th Anniversary Edition
Invites children of all faiths and backgrounds to encounter God through moments in
their own lives. 11 × 8½, 32 pp, Full-color illus., HC, 978-1-58023-195-8 **$17.95** *For ages 4 & up*

Also available: **God's Paintbrush Teacher's Guide** 8½ × 11, 32 pp, PB, 978-1-879045-57-6 **$8.95**

God's Paintbrush Celebration Kit
A Spiritual Activity Kit for Teachers and Students of All Faiths, All Backgrounds
Additional activity sheets available:
8-Student Activity Sheet Pack (40 sheets/5 sessions), 978-1-58023-058-2 **$19.95**
Single-Student Activity Sheet Pack (5 sessions), 978-1-58023-059-9 **$3.95**

Spiritual Biography—SkyLight Lives

SkyLight Lives reintroduces the lives and works of key spiritual figures of our time—people who by their teaching or example have challenged our assumptions about spirituality and have caused us to look at it in new ways.

   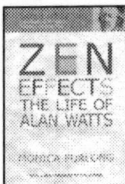

The Life of Evelyn Underhill
An Intimate Portrait of the Groundbreaking Author of *Mysticism*
by Margaret Cropper; Foreword by Dana Greene
Evelyn Underhill was a passionate writer and teacher who wrote elegantly on mysticism, worship, and devotional life.
6 x 9, 200 pp, 5 b/w photos, Quality PB, 978-1-893361-70-6 **$18.95**

Mahatma Gandhi: His Life and Ideas
by Charles F. Andrews; Foreword by Dr. Arun Gandhi
Examines from a contemporary Christian activist's point of view the religious ideas and political dynamics that influenced the birth of the peaceful resistance movement.
6 x 9, 336 pp, 5 b/w photos, Quality PB, 978-1-893361-89-8 **$18.95**

Simone Weil: A Modern Pilgrimage
by Robert Coles
The extraordinary life of the spiritual philosopher who's been called both saint and madwoman.
6 x 9, 208 pp, Quality PB, 978-1-893361-34-8 **$16.95**

Zen Effects: The Life of Alan Watts
by Monica Furlong
Through his widely popular books and lectures, Alan Watts (1915–1973) did more to introduce Eastern philosophy and religion to Western minds than any figure before or since.
6 x 9, 264 pp, Quality PB, 978-1-893361-32-4 **$16.95**

More Spiritual Biography

Bede Griffiths: An Introduction to His Interspiritual Thought
by Wayne Teasdale
The first study of his contemplative experience and thought, exploring the intersection of Hinduism and Christianity.
6 x 9, 288 pp, Quality PB, 978-1-893361-77-5 **$18.95**

The Soul of the Story: Meetings with Remarkable People
by Rabbi David Zeller
Inspiring and entertaining, this compelling collection of spiritual adventures assures us that no spiritual lesson truly learned is ever lost.
6 x 9, 288 pp, HC, 978-1-58023-272-2 **$21.99** *(a Jewish Lights book)*

Spiritual Poetry—The Mystic Poets

Experience these mystic poets as you never have before. Each beautiful, compact book includes: a brief introduction to the poet's time and place; a summary of the major themes of the poet's mysticism and religious tradition; essential selections from the poet's most important works; and an appreciative preface by a contemporary spiritual writer.

   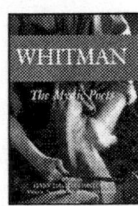

Hafiz: The Mystic Poets
Preface by Ibrahim Gamard
Hafiz is known throughout the world as Persia's greatest poet, with sales of his poems in Iran today only surpassed by those of the Qur'an itself. His probing and joyful verse speaks to people from all backgrounds who long to taste and feel divine love and experience harmony with all living things.
5 x 7¼, 144 pp, HC, 978-1-59473-009-2 **$16.99**

Hopkins: The Mystic Poets
Preface by Rev. Thomas Ryan, CSP
Gerard Manley Hopkins, Christian mystical poet, is beloved for his use of fresh language and startling metaphors to describe the world around him. Although his verse is lovely, beneath the surface lies a searching soul, wrestling with and yearning for God.
5 x 7¼, 112 pp, HC, 978-1-59473-010-8 **$16.99**

Tagore: The Mystic Poets
Preface by Swami Adiswarananda
Rabindranath Tagore is often considered the "Shakespeare" of modern India. A great mystic, Tagore was the teacher of W. B. Yeats and Robert Frost, the close friend of Albert Einstein and Mahatma Gandhi, and the winner of the Nobel Prize for Literature. This beautiful sampling of Tagore's two most important works, *The Gardener* and *Gitanjali,* offers a glimpse into his spiritual vision that has inspired people around the world.
5 x 7¼, 144 pp, HC, 978-1-59473-008-5 **$16.99**

Whitman: The Mystic Poets
Preface by Gary David Comstock
Walt Whitman was the most innovative and influential poet of the nineteenth century. This beautiful sampling of Whitman's most important poetry from *Leaves of Grass,* and selections from his prose writings, offers a glimpse into the spiritual side of his most radical themes—love for country, love for others, and love of Self.
5 x 7¼, 192 pp, HC, 978-1-59473-041-2 **$16.99**

Judaism / Christianity / Interfaith

Talking about God: Exploring the Meaning of Religious Life with Kierkegaard, Buber, Tillich and Heschel *by Daniel F. Polish, PhD*
Examines the meaning of the human religious experience with the greatest theologians of modern times. 6 x 9, 176 pp, HC, 978-1-59473-230-0 **$21.99**

Interactive Faith: The Essential Interreligious Community-Building Handbook
Edited by Rev. Bud Heckman with Rori Picker Neiss A guide to the key methods and resources of the interfaith movement. 6 x 9, 304 pp, HC, 978-1-59473-237-9 **$40.00**

The Jewish Approach to Repairing the World (*Tikkun Olam*)
A Brief Introduction for Christians *by Rabbi Elliot N. Dorff, PhD, with Reverend Cory Willson*
A window into the Jewish idea of responsibility to care for the world.
5½ x 8½, 256 pp, Quality PB, 978-1-58023-349-1 **$16.99** *(A book from Jewish Lights, SkyLight Paths' sister imprint)*

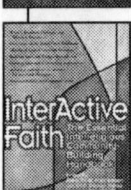

Modern Jews Engage the New Testament: Enhancing Jewish Well-Being in a Christian Environment *by Rabbi Michael J. Cook, PhD*
A look at the dynamics of the New Testament. 6 x 9, 416 pp, HC, 978-1-58023-313-2 **$29.99**
(A book from Jewish Lights, SkyLight Paths' sister imprint)

Disaster Spiritual Care: Practical Clergy Responses to Community, Regional and National Tragedy
Edited by Rabbi Stephen B. Roberts, BCJC, & Rev. Willard W.C. Ashley, Sr., DMin, DH
The definitive reference for pastoral caregivers of all faiths involved in disaster response.
6 x 9, 384 pp, Hardcover, 978-1-59473-240-9 **$40.00**

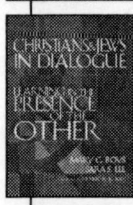

The Changing Christian World: A Brief Introduction for Jews
by Rabbi Leonard A. Schoolman 5½ x 8½, 176 pp, Quality PB, 978-1-58023-344-6 **$16.99**
(A book from Jewish Lights, SkyLight Paths' sister imprint)

The Jewish Connection to Israel, the Promised Land: A Brief Introduction for Christians *by Rabbi Eugene Korn, PhD* 5½ x 8½, 192 pp, Quality PB, 978-1-58023-318-7 **$14.99**
(A book from Jewish Lights, SkyLight Paths' sister imprint)

Christians and Jews in Dialogue: Learning in the Presence of the Other
by Mary C. Boys and Sara S. Lee; Foreword by Dorothy C. Bass Inspires renewed commitment to dialogue between religious traditions. 6 x 9, 240 pp, HC, 978-1-59473-144-0 **$21.99**

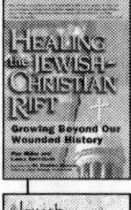

Healing the Jewish-Christian Rift: Growing Beyond Our Wounded History
by Ron Miller and Laura Bernstein; Foreword by Dr. Beatrice Bruteau
6 x 9, 288 pp, Quality PB, 978-1-59473-139-6 **$18.99**

Introducing My Faith and My Community: The Jewish Outreach Institute Guide for the Christian in a Jewish Interfaith Relationship *by Rabbi Kerry M. Olitzky* 6 x 9, 176 pp,
Quality PB, 978-1-58023-192-3 **$16.99** *(A book from Jewish Lights, SkyLight Paths' sister imprint)*

The Jewish Approach to God: A Brief Introduction for Christians *by Rabbi Neil Gillman*
5½ x 8½, 192 pp, Quality PB, 978-1-58023-190-9 **$16.95** *(A book from Jewish Lights, SkyLight Paths' sister imprint)*

Jewish Holidays: A Brief Introduction for Christians *by Rabbi Kerry M. Olitzky and Rabbi Daniel Judson* 5½ x 8½, 176 pp, Quality PB, 978-1-58023-302-6 **$16.99**
(A book from Jewish Lights, SkyLight Paths' sister imprint)

Jewish Ritual: A Brief Introduction for Christians
by Rabbi Kerry M. Olitzky and Rabbi Daniel Judson 5½ x 8½, 144 pp, Quality PB, 978-1-58023-210-4 **$14.99**
(A book from Jewish Lights, SkyLight Paths' sister imprint)

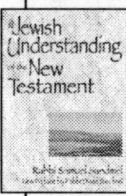

Jewish Spirituality: A Brief Introduction for Christians *by Rabbi Lawrence Kushner*
5½ x 8½, 112 pp, Quality PB, 978-1-58023-150-3 **$12.95** *(A book from Jewish Lights, SkyLight Paths' sister imprint)*

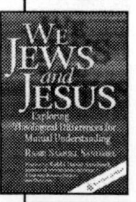

A Jewish Understanding of the New Testament *by Rabbi Samuel Sandmel;
new Preface by Rabbi David Sandmel* 5½ x 8½, 368 pp, Quality PB, 978-1-59473-048-1 **$19.99**

We Jews and Jesus: Exploring Theological Differences for Mutual Understanding
by Rabbi Samuel Sandmel; new Preface by Rabbi David Sandmel A Classic Reprint
6 x 9, 192 pp, Quality PB, 978-1-59473-208-9 **$16.99**

Show Me Your Way: The Complete Guide to Exploring Interfaith Spiritual Direction
by Howard A. Addison 5½ x 8½, 240 pp, Quality PB, 978-1-893361-41-6 **$16.95**

Spirituality of the Seasons

Autumn: A Spiritual Biography of the Season
Edited by Gary Schmidt and Susan M. Felch; Illustrations by Mary Azarian
Rejoice in autumn as a time of preparation and reflection. Includes Wendell Berry, David James Duncan, Robert Frost, A. Bartlett Giamatti, E. B. White, P. D. James, Julian of Norwich, Garret Keizer, Tracy Kidder, Anne Lamott, May Sarton.
6 x 9, 320 pp, 5 b/w illus., Quality PB, 978-1-59473-118-1 **$18.99**

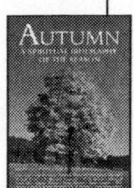

Spring: A Spiritual Biography of the Season
Edited by Gary Schmidt and Susan M. Felch; Illustrations by Mary Azarian
Explore the gentle unfurling of spring and reflect on how nature celebrates rebirth and renewal. Includes Jane Kenyon, Lucy Larcom, Harry Thurston, Nathaniel Hawthorne, Noel Perrin, Annie Dillard, Martha Ballard, Barbara Kingsolver, Dorothy Wordsworth, Donald Hall, David Brill, Lionel Basney, Isak Dinesen, Paul Laurence Dunbar. 6 x 9, 352 pp, 6 b/w illus., Quality PB, 978-1-59473-246-1 **$18.99**

Summer: A Spiritual Biography of the Season
Edited by Gary Schmidt and Susan M. Felch; Illustrations by Barry Moser
"A sumptuous banquet.... These selections lift up an exquisite wholeness found within an everyday sophistication."— ★ *Publishers Weekly* starred review
Includes Anne Lamott, Luci Shaw, Ray Bradbury, Richard Selzer, Thomas Lynch, Walt Whitman, Carl Sandburg, Sherman Alexie, Madeleine L'Engle, Jamaica Kincaid.
6 x 9, 304 pp, 5 b/w illus., Quality PB, 978-1-59473-183-9 **$18.99**
HC, 978-1-59473-083-2 **$21.99**

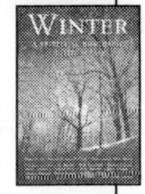

Winter: A Spiritual Biography of the Season
Edited by Gary Schmidt and Susan M. Felch; Illustrations by Barry Moser
"This outstanding anthology features top-flight nature and spirituality writers on the fierce, inexorable season of winter.... Remarkably lively and warm, despite the icy subject." — ★ *Publishers Weekly* starred review
Includes Will Campbell, Rachel Carson, Annie Dillard, Donald Hall, Ron Hansen, Jane Kenyon, Jamaica Kincaid, Barry Lopez, Kathleen Norris, John Updike, E. B. White.
6 x 9, 288 pp, 6 b/w illus., Deluxe PB w/flaps, 978-1-893361-92-8 **$18.95**

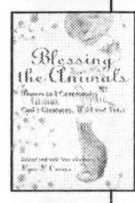

Spirituality / Animal Companions

Blessing the Animals: Prayers and Ceremonies to Celebrate God's Creatures, Wild and Tame *Edited by Lynn L. Caruso*
5¼ x 7¼, 256 pp, Quality PB, 978-1-59473-253-9 **$15.99**; HC, 978-1-59473-145-7 **$19.99**

Remembering My Pet: A Kid's Own Spiritual Workbook for When a Pet Dies
by Nechama Liss-Levinson, PhD, and Rev. Molly Phinney Baskette, MDiv; Foreword by Lynn L. Caruso
8 x 10, 48 pp, 2-color text, HC, 978-1-59473-221-3 **$16.99**

What Animals Can Teach Us about Spirituality: Inspiring Lessons from Wild and Tame Creatures *by Diana L. Guerrero* 6 x 9, 176 pp, Quality PB, 978-1-893361-84-3 **$16.95**

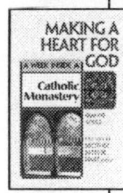

Spirituality—A Week Inside

Come and Sit: A Week Inside Meditation Centers
by Marcia Z. Nelson; Foreword by Wayne Teasdale
6 x 9, 224 pp, b/w photos, Quality PB, 978-1-893361-35-5 **$16.95**

Lighting the Lamp of Wisdom: A Week Inside a Yoga Ashram
by John Ittner; Foreword by Dr. David Frawley
6 x 9, 192 pp, 10+ b/w photos, Quality PB, 978-1-893361-52-2 **$15.95**

Making a Heart for God: A Week Inside a Catholic Monastery
by Dianne Aprile; Foreword by Brother Patrick Hart, OCSO
6 x 9, 224 pp, b/w photos, Quality PB, 978-1-893361-49-2 **$16.95**

Waking Up: A Week Inside a Zen Monastery
by Jack Maguire; Foreword by John Daido Loori, Roshi
6 x 9, 224 pp, b/w photos, Quality PB, 978-1-893361-55-3 **$16.95**; HC, 978-1-893361-13-3 **$21.95**

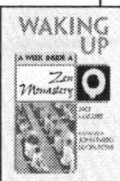

Sacred Texts—SkyLight Illuminations Series

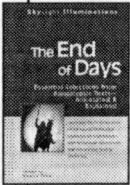

Offers today's spiritual seeker an accessible entry into the great classic texts of the world's spiritual traditions. Each classic is presented in an accessible translation, with facing pages of guided commentary from experts, giving you the keys you need to understand the history, context and meaning of the text. This series enables you, whatever your background, to experience and understand classic spiritual texts directly, and to make them a part of your life.

CHRISTIANITY

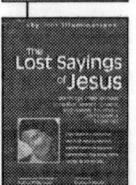

The End of Days: Essential Selections from Apocalyptic Texts—Annotated & Explained *Annotation by Robert G. Clouse*
Helps you understand the complex Christian visions of the end of the world.
5½ x 8½, 224 pp, Quality PB, 978-1-59473-170-9 **$16.99**

The Hidden Gospel of Matthew: Annotated & Explained
Translation & Annotation by Ron Miller
Takes you deep into the text cherished around the world to discover the words and events that have the strongest connection to the historical Jesus.
5½ x 8½, 272 pp, Quality PB, 978-1-59473-038-2 **$16.99**

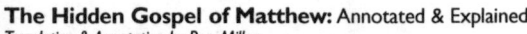

The Infancy Gospels of Jesus: Apocryphal Tales from the Childhoods of Mary and Jesus—Annotated & Explained *Stevan Davies; Foreword by A. Edward Siecienski*
A startling presentation of the early lives of Mary, Jesus, and other biblical figures that will amuse and surprise you. 5½ x 8½, 176 pp, Quality PB Original, 978-1-59473-258-4 **$16.99**

The Lost Sayings of Jesus: Teachings from Ancient Christian, Jewish, Gnostic and Islamic Sources—Annotated & Explained
Translation & Annotation by Andrew Phillip Smith; Foreword by Stephan A. Hoeller
This collection of more than three hundred sayings depicts Jesus as a Wisdom teacher who speaks to people of all faiths as a mystic and spiritual master.
5½ x 8½, 240 pp, Quality PB, 978-1-59473-172-3 **$16.99**

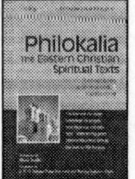

Philokalia: The Eastern Christian Spiritual Texts—Selections Annotated & Explained *Annotation by Allyne Smith; Translation by G. E. H. Palmer, Phillip Sherrard and Bishop Kallistos Ware*
The first approachable introduction to the wisdom of the Philokalia, which is the classic text of Eastern Christian spirituality.
5½ x 8½, 240 pp, Quality PB, 978-1-59473-103-7 **$16.99**

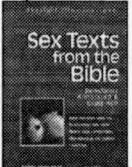

The Sacred Writings of Paul: Selections Annotated & Explained
Translation & Annotation by Ron Miller
Explores the apostle Paul's core message of spiritual equality, freedom and joy.
5½ x 8½, 224 pp, Quality PB, 978-1-59473-213-3 **$16.99**

Sex Texts from the Bible: Selections Annotated & Explained
Translation & Annotation by Teresa J. Hornsby; Foreword by Amy-Jill Levine
Offers surprising insight into our modern sexual lives.
5½ x 8½, 208 pp, Quality PB, 978-1-59473-217-1 **$16.99**

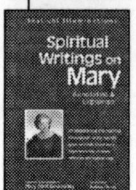

Spiritual Writings on Mary: Annotated & Explained
Annotation by Mary Ford-Grabowsky; Foreword by Andrew Harvey
Examines the role of Mary, the mother of Jesus, as a source of inspiration in history and in life today. 5½ x 8½, 288 pp, Quality PB, 978-1-59473-001-6 **$16.99**

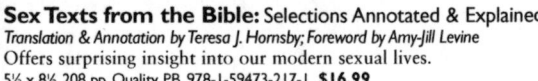

The Way of a Pilgrim: The Jesus Prayer Journey—Annotated & Explained
Translation & Annotation by Gleb Pokrovsky; Foreword by Andrew Harvey
This classic of Russian spirituality is the delightful account of one man who sets out to learn the prayer of the heart, also known as the "Jesus prayer."
5½ x 8½, 160 pp, Illus., Quality PB, 978-1-893361-31-7 **$14.95**

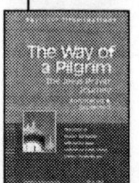

Sacred Texts—cont.

MORMONISM

The Book of Mormon: Selections Annotated & Explained
Annotation by Jana Riess; Foreword by Phyllis Tickle
Explores the sacred epic that is cherished by more than twelve million members of
the LDS church as the keystone of their faith.
5½ x 8½ , 272 pp, Quality PB, 978-1-59473-076-4 **$16.99**

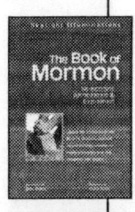

NATIVE AMERICAN

Native American Stories of the Sacred: Annotated & Explained
Retold & Annotated by Evan T. Pritchard
Intended for more than entertainment, these teaching tales contain elegantly simple illustrations of time-honored truths.
5½ x 8½, 272 pp, Quality PB, 978-1-59473-112-9 **$16.99**

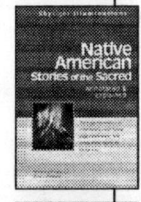

GNOSTICISM

Gnostic Writings on the Soul: Annotated & Explained
Translation & Annotation by Andrew Phillip Smith; Foreword by Stephan A. Hoeller
Reveals the inspiring ways your soul can remember and return to its unique,
divine purpose.
5½ x 8½, 144 pp, Quality PB, 978-1-59473-220-1 **$16.99**

The Gospel of Philip: Annotated & Explained
Translation & Annotation by Andrew Phillip Smith; Foreword by Stevan Davies
Reveals otherwise unrecorded sayings of Jesus and fragments of Gnostic mythology.
5½ x 8½, 160 pp, Quality PB, 978-1-59473-111-2 **$16.99**

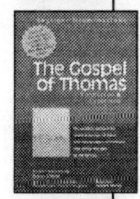

The Gospel of Thomas: Annotated & Explained
Translation & Annotation by Stevan Davies Sheds new light on the origins of Christianity and
portrays Jesus as a wisdom-loving sage.
5½ x 8½, 192 pp, Quality PB, 978-1-893361-45-4 **$16.99**

The Secret Book of John: The Gnostic Gospel—Annotated & Explained
Translation & Annotation by Stevan Davies The most significant and influential text of
the ancient Gnostic religion.
5½ x 8½, 208 pp, Quality PB, 978-1-59473-082-5 **$16.99**

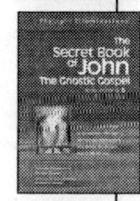

JUDAISM

The Divine Feminine in Biblical Wisdom Literature
Selections Annotated & Explained
Translation & Annotation by Rabbi Rami Shapiro; Foreword by Rev. Cynthia Bourgeault, PhD
Uses the Hebrew books of Psalms, Proverbs, Song of Songs, Ecclesiastes and Job,
Wisdom literature and the Wisdom of Solomon to clarify who Wisdom is.
5½ x 8½, 240 pp, Quality PB, 978-1-59473-109-9 **$16.99**

Ethics of the Sages: *Pirke Avot*—Annotated & Explained
Translation & Annotation by Rabbi Rami Shapiro Clarifies the ethical teachings of the
early Rabbis. 5½ x 8½, 192 pp, Quality PB, 978-1-59473-207-2 **$16.99**

Hasidic Tales: Annotated & Explained
Translation & Annotation by Rabbi Rami Shapiro
Introduces the legendary tales of the impassioned Hasidic rabbis, presenting them as
stories rather than as parables. 5½ x 8½, 240 pp, Quality PB, 978-1-893361-86-7 **$16.95**

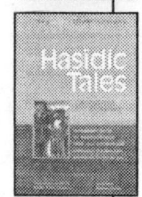

The Hebrew Prophets: Selections Annotated & Explained
Translation & Annotation by Rabbi Rami Shapiro; Foreword by Zalman M. Schachter-Shalomi
Focuses on the central themes covered by all the Hebrew prophets.
5½ x 8½, 224 pp, Quality PB, 978-1-59473-037-5 **$16.99**

Zohar: Annotated & Explained *Translation & Annotation by Daniel C. Matt*
The best-selling author of *The Essential Kabbalah* brings together in one place the most
important teachings of the Zohar, the canonical text of Jewish mystical tradition.
5½ x 8½, 176 pp, Quality PB, 978-1-893361-51-5 **$15.99**

Spirituality

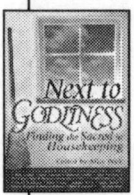

Next to Godliness: Finding the Sacred in Housekeeping
Edited and with Introductions by Alice Peck
Offers new perspectives on how we can reach out for the Divine.
6 x 9, 224 pp, Quality PB, 978-1-59473-214-0 **$19.99**

Bread, Body, Spirit: Finding the Sacred in Food
Edited and with Introductions by Alice Peck
Explores how food feeds our faith. 6 x 9, 224 pp, Quality PB, 978-1-59473-242-3 **$19.99**

Renewal in the Wilderness: A Spiritual Guide to Connecting with God
in the Natural World *by John Lionberger*
Reveals the power of experiencing God's presence in many variations of the natural world. 6 x 9, 176 pp, b/w photos, Quality PB, 978-1-59473-219-5 **$16.99**

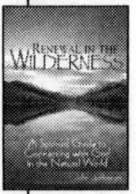

Honoring Motherhood: Prayers, Ceremonies and Blessings
Edited and with Introductions by Lynn L. Caruso
Journey through the seasons of motherhood. 5 x 7¼, 272 pp, HC, 978-1-59473-239-3 **$19.99**

Soul Fire: Accessing Your Creativity *by Rev. Thomas Ryan, CSP*
Learn to cultivate your creative spirit. 6 x 9, 160 pp, Quality PB, 978-1-59473-243-0 **$16.99**

Technology & Spirituality: How the Information Revolution Affects Our
Spiritual Lives *by Stephen K. Spyker* 6 x 9, 176 pp, HC, 978-1-59473-218-8 **$19.99**

Money and the Way of Wisdom: Insights from the Book of Proverbs
by Timothy J. Sandoval, PhD 6 x 9, 192 pp, Quality PB, 978-1-59473-245-4 **$16.99**

Awakening the Spirit, Inspiring the Soul
30 Stories of Interspiritual Discovery in the Community of Faiths
Edited by Brother Wayne Teasdale and Martha Howard, MD; Foreword by Joan Borysenko, PhD
6 x 9, 224 pp, HC, 978-1-59473-039-9 **$21.99**

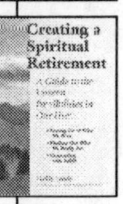

Creating a Spiritual Retirement: A Guide to the Unseen Possibilities in Our Lives
by Molly Srode 6 x 9, 208 pp, b/w photos, Quality PB, 978-1-59473-050-4 **$14.99**
HC, 978-1-893361-75-1 **$19.95**

Finding Hope: Cultivating God's Gift of a Hopeful Spirit
by Marcia Ford 8 x 8, 200 pp, Quality PB, 978-1-59473-211-9 **$16.99**

The Geography of Faith: Underground Conversations on Religious, Political and Social
Change *by Daniel Berrigan and Robert Coles* 6 x 9, 224 pp, Quality PB, 978-1-893361-40-9 **$16.95**

Jewish Spirituality: A Brief Introduction for Christians *by Lawrence Kushner*
5½ x 8½, 112 pp, Quality PB, 978-1-58023-150-3 **$12.95** *(A book from Jewish Lights, SkyLight Paths' sister imprint)*

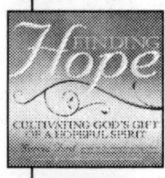

Journeys of Simplicity: Traveling Light with Thomas Merton, Bashō, Edward
Abbey, Annie Dillard & Others *by Philip Harnden*
5 x 7¼, 144 pp, Quality PB, 978-1-59473-181-5 **$12.99** 128 pp, HC, 978-1-893361-76-8 **$16.95**

Keeping Spiritual Balance As We Grow Older: More than 65 Creative Ways to
Use Purpose, Prayer, and the Power of Spirit to Build a Meaningful Retirement
by Molly and Bernie Srode 8 x 8, 224 pp, Quality PB, 978-1-59473-042-9 **$16.99**

Spirituality 101: The Indispensable Guide to Keeping—or Finding—Your Spiritual Life
on Campus *by Harriet L. Schwartz, with contributions from college students at nearly thirty campuses across the United States* 6 x 9, 272 pp, Quality PB, 978-1-59473-000-9 **$16.99**

Spiritually Incorrect: Finding God in All the Wrong Places *by Dan Wakefield; Illus. by
Marian DelVecchio* 5½ x 8½, 192 pp, b/w illus., Quality PB, 978-1-59473-137-2 **$15.99**

Spiritual Manifestos: Visions for Renewed Religious Life in America from Young
Spiritual Leaders of Many Faiths *Edited by Niles Elliot Goldstein; Preface by Martin E. Marty*
6 x 9, 256 pp, HC, 978-1-893361-09-6 **$21.95**

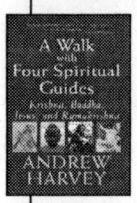

A Walk with Four Spiritual Guides: Krishna, Buddha, Jesus, and Ramakrishna
by Andrew Harvey 5½ x 8½, 192 pp, 10 b/w photos & illus., Quality PB, 978-1-59473-138-9 **$15.99**

What Matters: Spiritual Nourishment for Head and Heart
by Frederick Franck 5 x 7¼, 128 pp, 50+ b/w illus., HC, 978-1-59473-013-9 **$16.99**

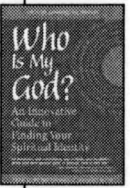

Who Is My God?, 2nd Edition: An Innovative Guide to Finding Your Spiritual Identity
Created by the Editors at SkyLight Paths 6 x 9, 160 pp, Quality PB, 978-1-59473-014-6 **$15.99**

Spiritual Practice

Soul Fire: Accessing Your Creativity *by Rev. Thomas Ryan, CSP*
Shows you how to cultivate your creative spirit as a way to encourage personal growth.
6 x 9, 160 pp, Quality PB, 978-1-59473-243-0 **$16.99**

Running—The Sacred Art: Preparing to Practice
by Dr. Warren A. Kay; Foreword by Kristin Armstrong
Examines how your daily run can enrich your spiritual life.
5½ x 8½, 160 pp, Quality PB, 978-1-59473-227-0 **$16.99**

Hospitality—The Sacred Art: Discovering the Hidden Spiritual Power
of Invitation and Welcome *by Rev. Nanette Sawyer; Foreword by Rev. Dirk Ficca*
Explores how this ancient spiritual practice can transform your relationships.
5½ x 8½, 192 pp, Quality PB, 978-1-59473-228-7 **$16.99**

Thanking & Blessing—The Sacred Art: Spiritual Vitality through
Gratefulness *by Jay Marshall, PhD; Foreword by Philip Gulley*
Offers practical tips for uncovering the blessed wonder in our lives—even in trying
circumstances. 5½ x 8½, 176 pp, Quality PB, 978-1-59473-231-7 **$16.99**

Everyday Herbs in Spiritual Life: A Guide to Many Practices
by Michael J. Caduto; Foreword by Rosemary Gladstar Explores the power of herbs.
7 x 9, 208 pp, 21 b/w illustrations, Quality PB, 978-1-59473-174-7 **$16.99**

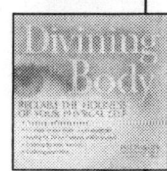

Divining the Body: Reclaim the Holiness of Your Physical Self *by Jan Phillips*
8 x 8, 256 pp, Quality PB, 978-1-59473-080-1 **$16.99**

Finding Time for the Timeless: Spirituality in the Workweek
by John McQuiston II Simple stories show you how refocus your daily life.
5½ x 6¼, 208 pp, HC, 978-1-59473-035-1 **$17.99**

The Gospel of Thomas: A Guidebook for Spiritual Practice
by Ron Miller; Translations by Stevan Davies
6 x 9, 160 pp, Quality PB, 978-1-59473-047-4 **$14.99**

Earth, Water, Fire, and Air: Essential Ways of Connecting to Spirit
by Cait Johnson 6 x 9, 224 pp, HC, 978-1-893361-65-2 **$19.95**

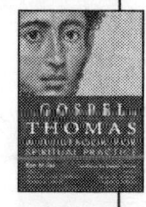

Labyrinths from the Outside In: Walking to Spiritual Insight—A Beginner's Guide
by Donna Schaper and Carole Ann Camp
6 x 9, 208 pp, b/w illus. and photos, Quality PB, 978-1-893361-18-8 **$16.95**

Practicing the Sacred Art of Listening: A Guide to Enrich Your Relationships
and Kindle Your Spiritual Life—The Listening Center Workshop
by Kay Lindahl 8 x 8, 176 pp, Quality PB, 978-1-893361-85-0 **$16.95**

Releasing the Creative Spirit: Unleash the Creativity in Your Life
by Dan Wakefield 7 x 10, 256 pp, Quality PB, 978-1-893361-36-2 **$16.95**

The Sacred Art of Bowing: Preparing to Practice
by Andi Young 5½ x 8½, 128 pp, b/w illus., Quality PB, 978-1-893361-82-9 **$14.95**

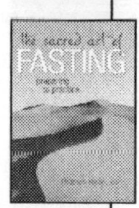

The Sacred Art of Chant: Preparing to Practice
by Ana Hernández 5½ x 8½, 192 pp, Quality PB, 978-1-59473-036-8 **$15.99**

The Sacred Art of Fasting: Preparing to Practice
by Thomas Ryan, CSP 5½ x 8½, 192 pp, Quality PB, 978-1-59473-078-8 **$15.99**

The Sacred Art of Forgiveness: Forgiving Ourselves and Others through God's Grace
by Marcia Ford 8 x 8, 176 pp, Quality PB, 978-1-59473-175-4 **$16.99**

The Sacred Art of Listening: Forty Reflections for Cultivating a Spiritual Practice
by Kay Lindahl; Illustrations by Amy Schnapper
8 x 8, 160 pp, b/w illus., Quality PB, 978-1-893361-44-7 **$16.99**

The Sacred Art of Lovingkindness: Preparing to Practice
by Rabbi Rami Shapiro; Foreword by Marcia Ford 5½ x 8½, 176 pp, Quality PB, 978-1-59473-151-8
$16.99

Sacred Speech: A Practical Guide for Keeping Spirit in Your Speech
by Rev. Donna Schaper 6 x 9, 176 pp, Quality PB, 978-1-59473-068-9 **$15.99**
HC, 978-1-893361-74-4 **$21.95**

Spirituality & Crafts

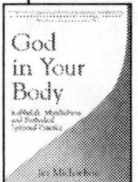

Contemplative Crochet: A Hands-On Guide for Interlocking Faith and Craft *by Cindy Crandall-Frazier; Foreword by Linda Skolnik*
Illuminates the spiritual lessons you can learn through crocheting.
7 x 9, 208 pp, b/w photographs, Quality PB, 978-1-59473-238-6 **$16.99**

The Knitting Way: A Guide to Spiritual Self-Discovery
by Linda Skolnik and Janice MacDaniels
Examines how you can explore and strengthen your spiritual life through knitting.
7 x 9, 240 pp, b/w photographs, Quality PB, 978-1-59473-079-5 **$16.99**

The Painting Path: Embodying Spiritual Discovery through Yoga, Brush and Color *by Linda Novick; Foreword by Richard Segalman*
Explores the divine connection you can experience through creativity.
7 x 9, 208 pp, 8-page full-color insert, plus b/w photographs
Quality PB, 978-1-59473-226-3 **$18.99**

The Quilting Path: A Guide to Spiritual Discovery through Fabric, Thread and Kabbalah *by Louise Silk*
Explores how to cultivate personal growth through quilt making.
7 x 9, 192 pp, b/w photographs and illustrations, Quality PB, 978-1-59473-206-5 **$16.99**

The Scrapbooking Journey: A Hands-On Guide to Spiritual Discovery
by Cory Richardson-Lauve; Foreword by Stacy Julian
Reveals how this craft can become a practice used to deepen and shape your life.
7 x 9, 176 pp, 8-page full-color insert, plus b/w photographs, Quality PB, 978-1-59473-216-4 **$18.99**

The Soulwork of Clay: A Hands-On Approach to Spirituality
by Marjory Zoet Bankson; Photographs by Peter Bankson
Takes you through the seven-step process of making clay into a pot, drawing parallels at each stage to the process of spiritual growth.
7 x 9, 192 pp, b/w photographs, Quality PB, 978-1-59473-249-2 **$16.99**

Kabbalah / Enneagram
(Books from Jewish Lights Publishing, SkyLight Paths' sister imprint)

God in Your Body: Kabbalah, Mindfulness and Embodied Spiritual Practice
by Jay Michaelson 6 x 9, 288 pp, Quality PB Original, 978-1-58023-304-0 **$18.99**

Cast in God's Image: Discover Your Personality Type Using the Enneagram and Kabbalah
by Rabbi Howard A. Addison 7 x 9, 176 pp, Quality PB, 978-1-58023-124-4 **$16.95**

Ehyeh: A Kabbalah for Tomorrow *by Dr. Arthur Green*
6 x 9, 224 pp, Quality PB, 978-1-58023-213-5 **$16.99**

The Enneagram and Kabbalah, 2nd Edition: Reading Your Soul
by Rabbi Howard A. Addison 6 x 9, 192 pp, Quality PB, 978-1-58023-229-6 **$16.99**

The Gift of Kabbalah: Discovering the Secrets of Heaven, Renewing Your Life on Earth
by Tamar Frankiel, PhD 6 x 9, 256 pp, Quality PB, 978-1-58023-141-1 **$16.95**
HC, 978-1-58023-108-4 **$21.95**

Kabbalah: A Brief Introduction for Christians
by Tamar Frankiel, PhD 5½ x 8½, 176 pp, Quality PB, 978-1-58023-303-3 **$16.99**

Zohar: Annotated & Explained *Translation and Annotation by Dr. Daniel C. Matt*
Foreword by Andrew Harvey 5½ x 8½, 176 pp, Quality PB, 978-1-893361-51-5 **$15.99**
(A book from Jewish Lights, SkyLight Paths' sister imprint)

Prayer / Meditation

Sacred Attention: A Spiritual Practice for Finding God in the Moment
by Margaret D. McGee
Framed on the Christian liturgical year, this inspiring guide explores ways to develop a practice of attention as a means of talking—and listening—to God.
6 x 9, 144 pp, HC, 978-1-59473-232-4 **$19.99**

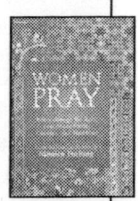

Women Pray: Voices through the Ages, from Many Faiths, Cultures and Traditions
Edited and with Introductions by Monica Furlong
5 x 7¼, 256 pp, Quality PB, 978-1-59473-071-9 **$15.99**

Women of Color Pray: Voices of Strength, Faith, Healing, Hope and Courage *Edited and with Introductions by Christal M. Jackson*
Through these prayers, poetry, lyrics, meditations and affirmations, you will share in the strong and undeniable connection women of color share with God.
5 x 7¼, 208 pp, Quality PB, 978-1-59473-077-1 **$15.99**

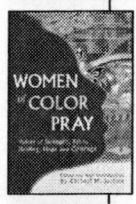

Secrets of Prayer: A Multifaith Guide to Creating Personal Prayer in Your Life *by Nancy Corcoran, CSJ*
This compelling, multifaith guidebook offers you companionship and encouragement on the journey to a healthy prayer life. 6 x 9, 160 pp, Quality PB, 978-1-59473-215-7 **$16.99**

Prayers to an Evolutionary God
by William Cleary; Afterword by Diarmuid O'Murchu
Inspired by the spiritual and scientific teachings of Diarmuid O'Murchu and Teilhard de Chardin, reveals that religion and science can be combined to create an expanding view of the universe—an evolutionary faith.
6 x 9, 208 pp, HC, 978-1-59473-006-1 **$21.99**

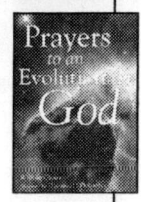

The Art of Public Prayer: Not for Clergy Only   *by Lawrence A. Hoffman*
6 x 9, 288 pp, Quality PB, 978-1-893361-06-5 **$18.99**

A Heart of Stillness: A Complete Guide to Learning the Art of Meditation
by David A. Cooper 5½ x 8½, 272 pp, Quality PB, 978-1-893361-03-4 **$16.95**

Meditation without Gurus: A Guide to the Heart of Practice
by Clark Strand 5½ x 8½, 192 pp, Quality PB, 978-1-893361-93-5 **$16.95**

Praying with Our Hands: 21 Practices of Embodied Prayer from the World's Spiritual Traditions *by Jon M. Sweeney; Photographs by Jennifer J. Wilson; Foreword by Mother Tessa Bielecki; Afterword by Taitetsu Unno, PhD*
8 x 8, 96 pp, 22 duotone photos, Quality PB, 978-1-893361-16-4 **$16.95**

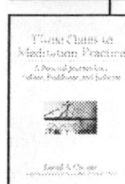

Silence, Simplicity & Solitude: A Complete Guide to Spiritual Retreat at Home
by David A. Cooper 5½ x 8½, 336 pp, Quality PB, 978-1-893361-04-1 **$16.95**

Three Gates to Meditation Practice: A Personal Journey into Sufism, Buddhism, and Judaism *by David A. Cooper* 5½ x 8½, 240 pp, Quality PB, 978-1-893361-22-5 **$16.95**

Prayer / M. Basil Pennington, OCSO

Finding Grace at the Center, 3rd Ed.: The Beginning of Centering Prayer   *with Thomas Keating, OCSO, and Thomas E. Clarke, SJ; Foreword by Rev. Cynthia Bourgeault, PhD*
A practical guide to a simple and beautiful form of meditative prayer.
5 x 7¼, 128 pp, Quality PB, 978-1-59473-182-2 **$12.99**

The Monks of Mount Athos: A Western Monk's Extraordinary Spiritual Journey on Eastern Holy Ground *Foreword by Archimandrite Dionysios*
Explores the landscape, the monastic communities, and the food of Athos.
6 x 9, 256 pp, 10+ b/w drawings, Quality PB, 978-1-893361-78-2 **$18.95**

Psalms: A Spiritual Commentary *Illustrations by Phillip Ratner*
Reflections on some of the most beloved passages from the Bible's most widely read book. 6 x 9, 176 pp, 24 full-page b/w illus., Quality PB, 978-1-59473-234-8 **$16.99**
HC, 978-1-59473-141-9 **$19.99**

The Song of Songs: A Spiritual Commentary *Illustrations by Phillip Ratner*
Explore the Bible's most challenging mystical text.
6 x 9, 160 pp, 14 b/w illus., Quality PB, 978-1-59473-235-3 **$16.99**; HC, 978-1-59473-004-7 **$19.99**

AVAILABLE FROM BETTER BOOKSTORES.
TRY YOUR BOOKSTORE FIRST.

About SKYLIGHT PATHS Publishing

SkyLight Paths Publishing is creating a place where people of different spiritual traditions come together for challenge and inspiration, a place where we can help each other understand the mystery that lies at the heart of our existence.

Through spirituality, our religious beliefs are increasingly becoming a part of our lives—rather than *apart* from our lives. While many of us may be more interested than ever in spiritual growth, we may be less firmly planted in traditional religion. Yet, we do want to deepen our relationship to the sacred, to learn from our own as well as from other faith traditions, and to practice in new ways.

SkyLight Paths sees both believers and seekers as a community that increasingly transcends traditional boundaries of religion and denomination—people wanting to learn from each other, *walking together, finding the way*.

For your information and convenience, at the back of this book we have provided a list of other SkyLight Paths books you might find interesting and useful. They cover the following subjects:

Buddhism / Zen	Global Spiritual	Monasticism
Catholicism	Perspectives	Mysticism
Children's Books	Gnosticism	Poetry
Christianity	Hinduism /	Prayer
Comparative	Vedanta	Religious Etiquette
Religion	Inspiration	Retirement
Current Events	Islam / Sufism	Spiritual Biography
Earth-Based	Judaism	Spiritual Direction
Spirituality	Kabbalah	Spirituality
Enneagram	Meditation	Women's Interest
	Midrash Fiction	Worship

Or phone, fax, mail or e-mail to: SKYLIGHT PATHS Publishing
Sunset Farm Offices, Route 4 • P.O. Box 237 • Woodstock, Vermont 05091
Tel: (802) 457-4000 • Fax: (802) 457-4004 • www.skylightpaths.com
Credit card orders: (800) 962-4544 (8:30AM–5:30PM ET Monday–Friday)
Generous discounts on quantity orders. SATISFACTION GUARANTEED. Prices subject to change.

For more information about each book,
visit our website at www.skylightpaths.com